Alicia's Daily Devotional Prayers

By: Alicia Sneij Perez

Acknowledgements

As with any project, rarely is it ever only from the efforts of one person but also the community that surrounds that person. The same applies to the writing of this prayer book- it started out with some friends I wanted to share a prayer with each day to encourage them on their walk as it encouraged me on my walk. Then the prayers were slowly extended to my faith community at my church, namely the Young Adult Group (YAG) at St. Augustine's Catholic Church in Miami, Florida. It was my friends at my church, along with my wonderful husband and my family that encouraged me to put all the prayers together into a book for others to enjoy. I hope you enjoy these prayers as much as I enjoyed writing them.

January 1

Father God, thank You for new beginnings. New beginnings allow us to look back and keep what we like and change what we didn't like- but it takes that time of reflection in order to do that effectively. New beginnings come in new relationships, both romantic and non-romantic relationships where we can learn from the mistakes we have made in previous relationships and try to fix it in any new relationships. New beginnings come in new jobs, where we are learning everything for the first time, meeting everyone for the first time and everything is a clean slate for us to learn and grow, reaching our fullest potential for Your glory. New beginnings come in the new year, where the previous year has come to an end and a new year has just begun with the opportunity for change, if we would just allow for it. Lord, may we embrace the new beginnings in our lives and reflect on what we can do to improve on what already is so that we can lead better and more fulfilling lives. In Your name we pray. Amen! :)

January 2

Father God, thank you for providing us the imagery of sheep following their shepherd wholeheartedly, knowing without a doubt that the shepherd truly loves them and cares for them. The shepherd wants the best for his sheep and not only protects his sheep from danger but seeks to bring them to green pastures and still waters. May we embrace this analogy in our life knowing that You are our Great Shepherd. May we navigate through this life knowing that You are leading us. Thank you for loving us and caring for us.

January 3

Father God, it is by your divine design that we go through this life uncertain of what happens next, continually seeking Your face in all that we do. You desire a relationship with us, continually conversing with us as we live our lives with you in mind. Please send us your Holy Spirit to guide our steps and lead us in the path of righteousness. Sanctify us each and every day as we become more and more like you, for You commanded us to become perfect as you, our Heavenly Father, is perfect. In the precious name of Jesus Christ. Amen!

January 4

Father God, we know that you hate division, yet as broken people, we keep dividing. Help us to restore unity in the Church once again as the Body of Christ, acting in harmony. Give us the strength to create peace when the enemy plots to create dissension. May we fight for unity and join forces with our brothers and sisters in Christ to be stronger together. In Jesus' name we pray, Amen!

"Jesus knew their thoughts and said to them, "Every kingdom divided against itself will be ruined, and every city or household divided against itself will not stand." -Matthew 12:25

January 5

Father God, thank You for being our foundation. Being mere humans, we are very weak and prone to stumble and fall. It is in those times of weakness that we look to You for the strength to carry on. Though we may struggle, we know that You are not looking down on us with contempt but with loving eyes waiting for us to get back up again. Just like a parent doesn't get mad when their child falls while taking their first steps, we know that You display the same loving disposition- anticipating for us to get right back up with a higher chance of going even further this time. Lord, may we not tire in this difficult journey of life but fall back on You when the going gets tough. Grant us the strength to keep pushing forward towards the finish line in this race of life. In Jesus' name, we pray. Amen! :)

January 6

Father God, we thank you that you never give up on us. It pleases you as our Heavenly Father to watch us grow in our faith but at the same time, you encourage us when we lose our footing and slip. May we know that You are cheering us on when we need to get back up, like a parent encourages their baby when they are learning to walk. Help us to understand our relationship with You as a father loves his child. Thank you for all the opportunities to seek Your face each and every day. In the name of Jesus. Amen!

January 7

Father God, thank you for the gift of prayer. Thank you that we can talk with you anytime of the day and share with you our joys and our sorrows- for we know You want to hear it all!! You already know what we are going to say but You want to hear it anyways- for our sake because a heart that is oriented to You is a joyful and cheerful heart. Help us to forgive those who have wronged us in the past so that we can pray effectively. We love you and praise you, O God. We lift up this day dedicated to Your will. In Jesus' name, Amen!

What is your relationship with prayer like? Do you enjoy engaging in prayer?

January 8

Father God, thank you for opening our eyes to Your saving truth. Help us to see your hand at work in our lives and to have faith that all things work out for our good. May we mindfully embrace the present but have our hearts set on what is to come. Allow us to indulge in the grace that You will grant us in the future. We thank you for the triune relationship between God the Father, Jesus the Son and the Holy Spirit, where we can relate to each in a unique and special way. We thank you for the graces You've bestowed upon us today and for the eyes to see it. In the precious name of Jesus, Amen!

January 9

Father God, thank you for all the blessings you have bestowed upon us today. May we have the spiritual eyes to see the blessings when they come our way. Lord, help us to commit every part of our lives to you so that we can see everything from Your perspective. Help us to find comfort in your embrace throughout the day, knowing that You are carrying us through. No matter what happens today, may we glorify Your name with our lives. In Jesus great name, Amen!

Do you acknowledge all the blessings you have in your life? How can you see life more with God's perspective?

January 10

Father God, help us put our lives into perspective. As the Creator of the universe where 1 million earths fit into 1 sun and the universe is endless, may we still feel small when we stand by the ocean. May You be big in comparison to our petty problems. No problem is too big for You. Restore in us awe and wonder at your works and who You are. Expand in us our faith to trust You in any which way our lives bend. Help us to love you with all of our hearts, minds and souls for that is what we were created for. We thank You for all that You are to us. In Jesus' holy name, Amen!

January 11

Father God, may we realize that our days on earth are numbered and that each day is a gift. Help us to embrace each and every moment as an opportunity to bring you glory. May we see your face in the faces that pass us by and help us to be more like You so that we can bring Christ to everyone that we encounter. Oh, how we long to be with you in Heaven- but until then we will serve faithfully here on earth. In the precious name of Jesus, Amen!

Do you acknowledge that your days are numbered? How does that change your perspective of life and how you approach your day?

January 12

Father God, thank you for this day and every day. Thank you for the storms that help us appreciate the sun. Thank you for humbling moments that keep our hearts from becoming prideful. Help us to see the day's events from Your perspective which will trivialize them- make them seem small compared to Your grand scheme design. May we see life through Your eyes and may we glorify You with our thoughts and actions. May the meditations of our hearts be pleasing to you, O Lord, our Rock and Redeemer. In Jesus' name. Amen!

January 13

Father God, thank you for your perfect Law. The Spirit of the Law is love and Jesus came down to fulfill the Law. The Law was established for us to show us that we are in need of a Savior. We are not capable of living a perfect life but that Christ Himself perfects us through the sanctification process. We pray that during trials, we can look up and say thank you for this perfecting and molding time. It is through the fire that our faith and character is strengthened. May we trust You with everything that we face on a day-to-day basis knowing that You hold everything in the palm of your hand. In the name of Jesus, we pray. Amen!

January 14

Father God, we can never fully fathom the extent of the love you have for us. In our limited state of being, we can only comprehend in a limited way from this side of eternity. Reveal to us Your unconditional love in little pockets each day so that we will continually seek Your Face. And grant us the strength to share the love that we receive with other people that desperately need that love. May our hearts be a river of love flowing in from your heart and flowing out to the hearts of others. Together we make up the body of Christ- may we continue to strive to be the hands and feet of a Jesus who loved the world. In the precious name of Jesus, Amen!

January 15

Father God, thank you for establishing one set of Truth that we can seek after with all our hearts and all come to one conclusion. You have planted Your Truth in our hearts which have made us restless until we find the source of that Truth, namely You. May we be good ambassadors of Your Truth to the world around us, representing Your love accurately and wholly. May we not leave any part of it out or add to it, for any omission or addition will not be the whole truth and nothing but the truth. We thank you for this day and we pray for the strength to live out our lives that are true to You, ourselves and the people around us. In Jesus' name, we pray. Amen!

January 16

Father God, thank you for Your sacrifice 2000 years ago where we can come to You for continued strength and energy to go about our days. We know our days are numbered and we want to spend our time here on earth in such a way that is holy and pleasing in Your sight. Help us with recurring sins that pop up along the way, giving us the strength to surrender them to You whenever they creep back into our lives. We were created to be perfect and each day is an opportunity for sanctification. We dedicate this and every day to You Lord- do with it as You please. In the name of Jesus, we pray. Amen!

January 17

Father God, thank you for this day where we are presented many opportunities to bring you glory. May we not be so caught up with our daily activities that we forget to spend some time with You and keep you in mind. Grant us the peace and assurance that You will do Your part as long as we do ours. And may we sit back and relax to see how the events of our lives unfold before our eyes. I pray that we can all trust You in your ways because Your ways are perfect. In the name of Jesus, amen!

Do you find yourself getting so caught up with all the petty details of your life and forget to spend important time with God? How can you be more mindful and change that?

January 18

Dear God, thanks. Thank you that Your Spirit provides freedom for our souls. Thank you for showing us Your Truth. Thank you for your grace that allows our hearts to accept You and not reject You. Thank you for sending Your Son, Jesus who came to us as one of us to show us the way to You. Thank you for His life-giving teachings that show us how to live a good and holy life. At the end of the day, Lord, may we see that there is much to be thankful for. As we rise and as we lay our heads down at night, may our hearts be full of gratitude towards that One who provides every good thing. In the name of Jesus, we pray. Amen!!

January 19

Dear God, thank you for commanding us to tithe and give generously. We know that You don't need the money but WE need to be reminded that You are the source of all that we have and it is You that provides for our needs. A cheerful and generous giver understands that we are not owners of what we have but managers. Help us to loosely hold on to the material blessings You have blessed us with so that we can be blessings to others. By your mercy and grace, You choose to pour out Your blessings through Your creation. Help us to not miss these opportunities- but that our eyes are peeled for the chances to serve and our hands are ready and willing to give. May we truly be the Hands and Feet of the One who made the Way. In Jesus' mighty name, we pray. Amen!!

January 20

Dear God, we are the pinnacle of Your Creation, truly made in Your image. Every human has Your imprint on his/her being. Your stamp of authentic Creation is on the face of every person we encounter. May we understand this and treat each and every person with the love that You have shown us. Help us to fight injustice around the world that belittles any one of Your children. Help us to genuinely love the homeless stranger down the street as one of Your dear children that needs help. May our hearts expand with the love that You have for Your children so that we do not neglect the needs of any one person. As You take care of our needs, help us be the hands and feet of Your Son to meet the needs of others. May the words of our mouths and the meditations of our hearts be acceptable to You, O Lord, our rock and our redeemer. In the name of Jesus, amen!

Do you acknowledge the beauty of the human life? How can we embrace every person's life more fully, both the born and unborn person? How can we see Jesus in the homeless person struggling to get their life in order?

"So God created mankind in his own image,
   in the image of God he created them;
     male and female he created them." -Genesis 1:27

January 21

Dear God, as humility is the root of all virtue, may you unleash the floodgates of humility on our lives. Help us to see how we can be humble in each and every situation- guiding us to act according to Your Will. Let us recognize how we can build up and not tear down, how we can encourage rather discourage, how we can lend a helping hand and accept a helping hand when in need. In the same token, as pride is the root of all vice, may You lock the door to moments of pride. And when these moments come our way, grant us the strength to swallow our pride and yield to Your life-giving spirit. Grant us the humility to seek Your Face every second of every day. In Jesus' name, Amen!

January 22

Father God, thank you for yet another day to love You and Your people. Help us to love those around us with unconditional love and to serve their needs. As we all know, our lives are not summed up by a compilation of achievements but of how we have impacted other people's lives. People will not remember how much we have accomplished but by how much we've loved. Let us meditate on this truth today so that we will take steps towards loving people and be less focused on what doesn't really matter. Nurture our love for You so that it will overflow into love for others. We pray this in Jesus' sweet name. Amen!

January 23

Dear God, may we never forget the mercies and graces that You pour on us daily. Restore in us the joy of Your salvation and grant us the ability to see Your Hand at work all around us. May we be satisfied with what You have blessed us with and not compare what You have given us to what You have given to our neighbors. Remind us that we are fearfully and wonderfully made in Your image and that we have a purpose specially designed for us. We thank You that all that we need in this life is Your presence so that we don't need to toil and strive for anything else. Many things in this world promise life but we all know that the source of true life resides in Your Son, Jesus Christ. May gratitude always dwell in our hearts and come out as praise. In Jesus' mighty name. Amen!

What mercies and graces must we remind ourselves today?

January 24

Father God, thank you for giving us guidelines in Your Word to help us build a foundation for our lives that will withstand any blows of storms and trials that pass through. You didn't say that You will take away the storms and trials but that You will teach us how to build on solid Rock so that when the storms pass, we will still be standing strong. And even more, teach us how to dance through life's storms, twirling and embracing the rain that drops on our face. Life is not about waiting for the storms to pass but about learning how to dance in the rain. With our eyes fixed on You, Lord, may we never be swayed by the currents of life but that we can have the faith to step out of the boat and walk on the water with You. In Your name we pray, amen!

January 25

Dear God, thank you for reaching out to us in our less than desirable state of unholiness and uncleanliness. We have it planted in our hearts to strive and achieve perfection but we cannot without the aid of Your Holy Spirit. Help us to look more and more like You and less like us. In our finite and limited selves, unleash the power of Your Spirit in our lives, where we can trust You no matter where the road may bend and love others with a love that can only originate from a supernatural source. Lord, take this day and every day to glorify You in all that we think, say and do. May we partake in the day's activities but mindful of You in all of our ways. In Jesus' name, we pray. Amen!

January 26

Jesus, thank You for the promise You made to Your disciples that You will be with us till the end of time. That means that You are walking with us and even carrying us through the trials and the storms that we may face in our lives. Grant us the peace that You had while sleeping in the stern of the boat while Your disciples were frantic during the storm. Grow our faith in You and help us to believe with all of our hearts the promises that You gave to us, promises of goodwill and a safe landing. May we never leave Your side as we go through trials and tribulations but cling ever so tightly to Your hem. Lord, we lift up this day and every day to You- may we act in accordance to Your will. In the precious name of Jesus, Amen! :)

January 27

Father God, thank You for caring so deeply for us. Who are we that You are even mindful of us? Help us to never doubt Your unconditional love for us and when we do, give us the strength to reject that ever so blatant lie whispered into our ears by the enemy. If we are truly Your beloved people, help us to believe it. You love us inside and out, knowing every little detail of our imperfections and limitations. You love us for who we really are so we don't have to hide any part of the personality You specifically designed to bring You glory. May we fully embrace who you crafted us to be, bringing a smile to Your face every time we live out the lives You have planned for us. In the precious name of Jesus, Amen!

January 28

Dear God, thank You for the Church that You have established that helps us navigate through this life. Without a shepherd herding us in the right direction, we can easily be led astray. With great role models that came before us, like Peter, Paul and the rest of the saints, may we be bold witnesses of Your mercy and goodness to the people around us. May we faithfully represent who You really are in our lives. You are not just something we put in a box and push to the side but rather a relationship that permeates through every aspect of our lives. May our faith in You grow ever deeper each and every passing day. In Jesus' name, Amen!

What is your relationship with the Church and the Saints? Do they help you walk closer with Christ?

January 29

Jesus, You promised to never leave us. Help us to feel Your presence by our side during the times we go through trials and temptations. Grant us the faith to believe in Your promises, that You love us and will never forsake us. You are our shepherd and thus we shall not want. You lead us beside the still waters and make us lie down on green pastures. Grant us peace everlasting as we dwell in the house of The Lord all the days of our lives. In Jesus' mighty name, Amen!

January 30

Lord Jesus, thank You for forgiving us our sins. You not only provided healing for our physical bodies but You also healed our souls. You break chains that hold us back from what You truly want us to be. You provide unity of our mind, body and soul. Lord, we know that in order to make a difference in this world, the change has to start in us. We ask that You would transform our hearts and minds to produce thoughts that are holy and pleasing to You, O Lord. We pray that You would guide our steps so that we are walking toward Your glory and not away. We ask that You would work through our hands so that they can provide healing and not destruction to the people around us. Help us to see You in every face we see so that we would be moved to love our brothers and sisters and treat them accordingly. We thank you for your mercy and grace that provides us the strength to push on every single day of our lives until we join You in glory with our Father in heaven. In Your precious name, we pray. Amen!!

What sins has God forgiven you? What chains have been broken in your life?

Dear God, thank you for all the blessings You shower upon us every day. May we never forget them but wake up each morning with a gratitude that fills our hearts. Help us to grasp the unrepeatableness and uniqueness of our existence. There will never be another person exactly like ourselves and that we have something special and unique to contribute to the world around us. Help us to embrace the love that You have for each person and make it sufficient for our joy that radiates outwards. Your love is all we need so we don't have to strive for anything else to fill that "God-shaped" void in our hearts. May we sacrificially love those around us as You have first loved us. In Jesus' name, Amen!

What unique characteristic or trait that you or someone else have that you should start appreciating and thanking God for today?

"The Lord has done it this very day; let us rejoice today and be glad." -Psalm 118:24

February 1

Lord Jesus, You have the power to break chains in our lives that hold us back from the potential that You have for us. You did it back then with the 2 demon possessed men and You are still doing it today. Thank you for granting us the strength to cling to Your side and resist temptation when it comes our way. Help us to remain pure and holy, always striving to be the people You have created us to be. Thank you for loving us into existence. May we fully love You and the people around us. In Jesus' name we pray. Amen! :)

February 2

Father God, we know that You take the ordinary and make them extraordinary for Your glory. You don't need our capabilities but our availability for You to work in our lives. Help us to humble ourselves and allow You to do the work You have planned for us during our time here on earth. May we not miss any opportunity for us to be Your hands and feet, tending to the needs of the people around us. Help us to not feel that our contribution is trivial but powerful when used by You. Grant us energy and enthusiasm this day and every day to carry out the work You have blessed us with, for we know that anything that we do, whether mundane or exciting, is meant to bring You glory. In Jesus' name we pray. Amen!

How has God taken the ordinary and made it extraordinary in your life?

February 3

Father God, though we are called to work, help us to remember that all that we have is provisioned to us by You. What we have is because You allow us to have it and whatever You have blessed us with should be a blessing to others. Humble us so that we will not grow attached to earthly possessions but keep our eyes fixed on heavenly attributes. Allow us to loosely hold onto the things of this world so that when they are taken away, we can let go of them easily. Create in us a grateful heart that praises You when You give and when You take away. Help us to serve without the expectation of anything in return. Help us to give wholeheartedly without a hidden agenda. And grant us the humility to receive when someone wants to use their blessings to bless our lives. In Jesus' name, we pray. Amen!

What is your relationship to earthly possessions like? Are you loosely attached or very attached? Are you able to praise God when He gives and when He takes away?

February 4

Father God, life may be difficult but it's certainly worth it. Help us not to dwell on the chaos around us but on Your goodness and mercy. Help us to not see life as a cruise ship where everything is fine and dandy but as a war ship where we are armored, armed and ready to withstand the fiery arrows of the enemy. Everyday is a day where the enemy is a prowling lion ready to devour his prey. Grant us the strength to meditate on Your promises daily to equip us with the proper tools to stand strong. Help us to "look back and thank you; look forward and trust You; look around and serve You; look within and find You". Wherever we look, may we find You there in the midst of it all- in the chaos and in the order- may our hearts be stilled with peace. In the sweet name of Jesus, we pray. Amen! :)

How has your life been more like a battleship than a cruise ship? Are you prepared to take on the day of battle each morning?

February 5

Father God, no two days are the same. Who we are today is different from the person we were yesterday and will be different from the person we will be tomorrow. If we are not running towards You, we are drifting away from You like a boat drifts away from the dock in the ocean. May our hearts be ever ready for what You have planned for us today, to make us grow and look more like You. You could have easily snapped Your heavenly fingers and eliminated all sin, granted us all salvation and allowed us to be in heaven with You today; but in all Your divine mercy and goodness, You have chosen this long and arduous path of sanctification where You have promised to walk beside us as we take steps to look more and more like Your Son. May we never forget our purpose here on earth, which is to glorify You in ALL that we do and to become holy as You our Father is holy in heaven. Grant this day a fresh mindset to take on the challenges You have in store and make every situation pleasing and glorifying to You. In Jesus' mighty name. Amen!

How do you compare to yourself 5- 10 years ago? Are you closer to God or further away?

February 6

Father God, just as the Psalmist King David requested of You, remind us that our days on earth are numbered. We are not here forever but what we do here will have everlasting effects. Whether we decide to love You and follow You will decide the fate of our eternity. May we not be slothful in loving and serving You, giving it our all until our last breath where we will be reunited with You. Help us to not live for ourselves but for You and for others. May we never miss an opportunity to serve a neighbor in need. May we make every moment count and strive for goodness. Grant us the strength to finish the race of life with utmost determination and diligence, awaiting for the day where we meet You face to face and hear the ever-so-sweet words: "Well done, good and faithful servant". We pray this in Jesus' powerful name. Amen!

Are you mindful that our days are limited but they have eternal effects? How can we make the most out of every day, with eternity in mind?

"Show me, Lord, my life's end
   and the number of my days;
   let me know how fleeting my life is." – Psalm 39:4

February 7

Dear God, please forgive us when we are not grateful for what You have given us. Sometimes we like to play God and tell You how things should be. But You intentionally do things in a certain way so that we can continually run to You and fully understand what it means for Your Grace to be sufficient for us. Grow in us a sense of overwhelming gratitude so that it manifests as praise in our hearts. May the first and last words that come out of our mouth in the mornings and when we lay down to rest be praise for Your mercy and goodness. Jesus has performed many miracles to show us how much You care for us. As Jesus continually performs miracles in our lives, may it strengthen our trust in Your providence for our lives. In Jesus' mighty name, we pray. Amen!

How have you tried to play God and tell Him how things should go? What areas in your life can you be more grateful?

February 8

Dear God, as the root of all vice is pride and the queen of all virtue is humility, eradicate all that makes us prideful and grow in us our humility. We know very well that You oppose the proud but give grace to the humble (Proverbs 3:34). Help us to see our limitations as avenues for Your grace to intervene and satisfy. Show us our rightful place in our relationship with you as we walk humbly with You by our side (Micah 6:8). Thank you for our beautiful relationship with you as a Father/child dyad- where we can fully rest knowing that our Heavenly Father is watching over and taking care of us. Grant us humility so that we can accept the fact that we cannot control everything and have to rely solely on You. And with that truth in our lives, we can be liberated from the bondage of control. Help us to dance with Your Spirit as it guides us through our lives. In Jesus' precious name, Amen!

How has pride and humility played in your life? How can you expand on humility and reduce in pride?

"Whoever derides their neighbor has no sense,
but the one who has understanding holds their tongue."
– Proverbs 11:12

Father God, while You are a just God, You are also a merciful God. As Your children, You want us to imitate You when You tell us that You want mercy not sacrifice. Father, when someone wrongs us, may we find it in us to forgive them even though they don't deserve forgiveness. As much as we deserved death for all of our sins, You decided to have mercy and pardon our sins through the sacrifice of Your Son, Jesus Christ. And to top it all off, You shower us with Your grace, granting to us what we don't deserve, namely salvation and the gifts of the Spirit. Thank You for being the merciful and gracious God that we so willingly serve and glorify with our lives. Help us today and every day to look more and more like You in our thoughts, words and actions. We love You and praise You. In Jesus' name we pray. Amen! :)

Who has wronged you in your past that you should let go and forgive? What can you do to shower love and blessings on that person instead of harboring unforgiveness?

Father God, we cannot live this life alone. We know that You created us for relationships for a reason; You want us to love You and love others. Help us to be there for a neighbor when they are hurting or in need. Use the trying times that You have allowed us to go through to be something that we can use to help others as they walk through their times of trials. Help us not to lose faith when we cannot see the sun shining behind the clouds. Remind us that You are in control, even when it doesn't seem like it. Grant us the strength to persevere to the end with great determination to do Your will in our lives. And help us to know what is Your will in our lives as we take a baby step towards where we feel Your Spirit nudging us. Thank you for being so gentle and kind as we go through this sanctification process called life. And we know that You are there with us every step of the way. In Jesus' name, we pray. Amen!!

Who in your life is going through a difficult time that you can give more attention and help?

Father God, thank You for waking us up this morning happy, healthy and alive for we know that this is not the case for everyone. Help us to count our blessings rather than dwell on what upsets us. Life is too short to focus on energy robbers but we should invest our precious time and energy into what pleases You. At the end of the day, the goal of our lives is to bring You glory by loving You and loving others. In every situation that we encounter, may we assess our response by the caliber that would bring You the most glory. How can we love You and the people You put around us the most? Even if it takes a stab at our pride, grant us the strength to push past the situation towards the sun that is shining behind the clouds. In every situation, may we see the silver lining and thus see You. In Jesus' precious name we pray. Amen!

What energy robbers have you been allowing to steal your joy, peace and happiness?

February 12

Father God, You created us to be relational beings, having a relationship with you and with the people around us. Help us not to take these relationships for granted but actively looking for ways we can serve one another. Help us to be more aware of Your presence in our lives, as we can go about our day not acknowledging You once. Just like we hate to be ignored, You very much do not like to be ignored. Help us to be mindful of You in all our ways. In this community that You have blessed us with, let us not be impatient, jealous, angry or disrespectful but rather display all the fruits of the Spirit including love, peace, joy and patience. May people know that we follow You by our fruits, bringing glory to Your name. Bring our hearts today and every day in unity with all the saints in praise for Your holy name. In Jesus' sweet name, we pray. Amen!

How is your daily communication with God? Are you continually acknowledging God's presence in your life or does He take the sidelines sometimes?

February 13

Father God, You never fail to provide even when we accuse You of not meeting our needs. Just like the Israelites in Egypt, we complain and complain but never see the blessing of You delivering us from bondage of slavery. Just like a loving father, You don't hesitate to discipline us with the rod to make us worthy children. Though we kick and flail as little children when we don't get our way, teach us to trust You in all of Your ways. Though we may not understand everything, help us to take Your hand and go wherever You lead us. In a life where we cannot see where the road bends, there is nothing left for us to do but to trust You. So, today and every-day, help us to be faithful in what You have entrusted us to do today and leave the rest of the details up to You. We thank You this day for Your loving grace and supplication. In Jesus' name, we pray. Amen!

What "needs" do you have that you accuse God not meeting? What blessings do you have that you have not thanked God for today?

February 14

Father God, thank You for the gift of love. The concept of love is so intangible and escaping but it is the single most beautiful aspect of a human being that separates us from the rest of creation. We were created to love and to be loved. Loved by our creator God and by our fellow neighbors. But love is only perfect when it's freely reciprocated. Though we were created for perfect love, we are not perfect and cannot love completely. This is when sin comes into play- damaging relationships and destroying the beautiful community we're designed to have with one another. Although we were designed to receive perfect love, may we learn to receive that complete love from our Heavenly Father and not depend on our fellow neighbors to love perfectly because they most likely will not. May we focus rather in perfecting our love towards our father and our neighbor as we graciously receive love back in any way that it comes. In Jesus' sweet name we pray. Amen! :)

What is your understanding of love? Have you been hurt before receiving imperfect love? How can we focus on loving more perfectly?

"Love is patient, love is kind. It does not envy, it does not boast, it is not proud." - 1 Corinthians 13:4

February 15

Father God, thank You for being a merciful and just God. Taking on our sin and giving us eternal life, we are eternally grateful. May we focus on those beautiful aspects of life rather than get caught up with temporal issues. May we be "eternity" driven, fueling us to live for Your glory. As one act creates a habit, a habit creates character and character creates a destiny, may we never underestimate the importance of each and every thought, word and deed- for it is on these small factors our lives are based on. Thank you for being the God that You are- a God of love, mercy and goodness. May we fixate our gaze on all that You are and be less focused on us. In Jesus' mighty name, Amen!

What "small" bad habit do we do on a daily basis? What good habit can we replace it with?

February 16

Father God, at the end of time, we know that we will give an account for all that we are responsible for here on earth. Everything that we do today in the short span of our lifetime will have eternal effects. Help us not to get flustered by trivial disturbances in our lives. These are all simply distractions from the important mission in life. When we face technical problems or we grow impatient, grant us the grace to step back, relax and surrender whatever it is that frustrates us. With our vocations being our missions and heaven our goal- may we never lose sight of heaven, our goal. Thank you for the saints and the angels that help us on a daily basis as we tread through the uncertain waters of life. We ask that You would grant us peace and serenity today and always. In Jesus' name, amen! :)

What distraction in life have we become impatient with that has taken our focus away from our goal?

February 17

Father God, often times we take for granted all that You have blessed us with, especially our loved ones. As the people of Nazareth didn't appreciate Jesus when He went back to His hometown, so can we do the same with our terms of familiarity. Open our eyes to the truth of reality and allow us to fully appreciate and grasp the integrity of what is before us. May we always see the beauty that radiates all around us. Help us to recognize truth when we see it and love when it's presented to us. We pray that You would strengthen the familial bonds within parents and children, brothers and sisters, immediate family and extended family, blood family and in-laws. Many times, the ones we hurt the most are the ones we love the most. Help us to break this habit and embrace the graces showered on us daily. In the name of Jesus, we pray. Amen! :)

How is your relationship with your family? Do you show the same love you do for friends and strangers as you do to your family?

February 18

Father God, each and every day, we are faced with competing temptations that grab our attention. They promise life but they fail because they are counterfeit. Help us to identify and remove the temptations in our lives that prevent us from being fully devoted to You. You are the true Bread of Life, that provides complete satisfaction. Help us to strive for You in all that we do. Help us to die to ourselves so that we can live in You. Our lives are not meant for us, they are meant to bring You greater glory. Take us off of the pedestal of our lives and place You back on Your rightful throne. Only then will we fully live, is when we fully die to our sinful nature. Today, please help us to fixate our eyes on You and nothing but You so that we can strive for the goal and not be distracted. In Jesus' mighty name, we pray. Amen!!

What counterfeit temptations have been popping up in your life?

Father God, it is easy for us to lose sight of You and to look around at all the wind and rain wailing around us. It is during these times of storm and doubt that we, like Peter, must cling ever more tightly to You. When everything seems to be crumbling around us, may we stand on the Rock foundation where we build our faith on. You never promised us that we will never face drought or storm but that You will always be with us as we walk through with confidence. And as our faith is strengthened with every difficult time, may we use those testimonies to reach out to our brothers and sisters, guiding them ever more closely to You. As the true source of Life, may we continually come back to You for rejuvenation. In Jesus' mighty name, we pray. Amen!

What storms have you gone through in your life? Did you keep your eyes focused on Jesus or were you focused on everything that was happening around you? How can your storm help others going through similar situations?

February 20

Father God, in the midst of trying times when everything seems to be saying one thing, may we always hear the still small voice that whispers Your promises to our hearts. When the 12 scouts went to reconnoiter the promised land, 10 were frightened and retracted at the sight of giants while 2 held tightly to Your promises and believed that You would carry them through. Today as we face all kinds of different "giants" in our lives, may we not cower but stand strong for we know we are on our Father's shoulders. In the midst of heavy darkness, may we be more aware of Your soothing presence that sheds light enough for us to tread forward. We know that although we will face trials and difficulties, we are comforted to know that You are right there with us, holding our hand- and we thank you for that. In Jesus' precious name we pray. Amen!! :)

———————————————

What area in your life seems to be frightening but should be holding strong to God's promises?

February 21

Father God, it's easy for us to grow numb to the mundane tasks we do each and every day. May we not fall asleep to Your glory that You prepare for us anew every morning. May our eyes be in tune to the many miracles You perform for us, be it the very fact our eyes open this morning and we regain consciousness, the flowers that bloom and blossom just for Your glory, the birds that chirp and provide music to our ears. May we wake up each morning with the anticipation to immerse ourselves in Your glory. As we look at the world around us, may we see countless miracles to marvel at. And as we think of Your magnificence, may we be filled with awe-inspiring wonder. In Jesus' name, we pray. Amen!!

Are you in-tune to the countless miracles that happen daily? How can you immerse yourself more in the beauty of life?

Lord Jesus, You said that faith the size of a mustard seed is more than enough to move mountains in our lives. Help us to not despair when we encounter yet another mountain in our life but to look up and know where we get our strength from. May we give thanks even for the obstacles for they are part of the sanctification process. While our vocation is our mission, heaven is our goal- may we never lose sight of You standing at the gate of heaven with Your arms stretched out wide to embrace us as we cross over into eternity. Thank You, Lord for the hope You replenish in our hearts each and every day. May we wake up each morning with the energy, strength and faith to take on any mountain that comes our way. Jesus, we believe in Your saving grace but help us with our unbelief. In Your precious name, we pray. Amen!

:)

What new mountain have you encountered recently? Do you have the faith, energy and strength to conquer it?

February 23

Father God, as a grain of wheat must die when it is thrown to the ground in order to produce greater life, help us to die to ourselves in order to give way to the life that is promised in Your will for us. As we are finite and small, and our thoughts are not like Your thoughts, help us to accept and follow Your lead. As little immature children who are rebellious to the guidance of their parents, we tend to kick and scream when we don't get our way. Lord, gently discipline us and mold us into the mature Christian that can stand with confidence in Your love. When life doesn't seem to go the way we would like it to go, may we look up and smile only to see You smiling back down on us. Grant us the strength to die to ourselves each and every day to give rise to You and all that You have planned for us. May we fully embrace this paradox of life: we must die in order to live. Help us to hope in Your Son and to follow joyfully the path which You have chosen. In Jesus' sovereign name, we pray. Amen! :)

In what ways have you "died" to yourself in order to bring new life?

February 24

Father God, You never fail to flip our worldview upside down. As leaders and people with power and authority are known to be admired in society, You make the claim that a mere child is the greatest in the kingdom of heaven. An innocent child without any power or authority has complete trust and dependence on the providence of the parents. As adults we have lost our trust and dependence over the years, feeling that we have to take matters into our own hands. Help us to re-establish that trust knowing that You are holding our hand as we walk through the valley of death. Help us to close our eyes when we retire for the day and lay down to rest, knowing full well that You have everything under control. Show us this simple truth You wish for us to know so that it marinates and seeps deep into our hearts as we trust in every direction You wish to take us. Instill once again the awe and wonder of the world around us invigorating our excitement for life. Build that trust relationship between a Father and child in us so that no matter where the road of life bends, we can have that assurance that Daddy has got everything under control. Help us to become great by humbling ourselves and adopting the mindset of a child once again. In Jesus' sweet name, we pray.
Amen!

Do you remember how it was like to be a child? How can we be more like children again?

Father God, we know that our brothers and sisters, as mere and finite humans, will fail us in one way or another. Moreover, they will even sin against us and we are called to forgive and love them. Lord, in times when we or our brothers and sisters fall short in our relationships, grant us patience and peace as we seek to reconcile the situation. Show us how we can do our part to show love as our brother or sister is struggling to find their way. May we be instruments of peace rather than avenues of fuel that aggravate the situation. And when it is us that falls short, grant us the humility to accept and rectify the situation. When it is sin that we are dealing with, may we not set any obstacle for our brother or sister to see their wrongdoing and facilitate the path to reconciliation with us and with You. Thank You, Lord, for finding us worthy to participate in Your mission of purifying and sanctifying Your people through Your people. And during this process of sanctification, may we never lose sight of what's most important- You. In Jesus' mighty name, we pray. Amen!! :)

How have your brothers and sisters failed you in your life? What have you done to rectify the situation? Have you forgiven them and shown them love anyways?

February 26

Father God, it's not difficult to look at the world around us and point out what is not meant to be. Just like in holy matrimony, You created marriage as a covenant for a man and woman to be joined together to demonstrate to the rest of the world the love You have for us. But now our marriages are failing and falling apart, becoming perversely thwarted, deviating from its original design and no longer accurately depicting the relationship You have with us. Help us to preserve the integrity of this beautiful union between men and women in any way we can. Help us to love the people that do not see marriage as a holy sacrament but as a mere human construction that can be tampered with and modified to fit our desired lifestyles. For those of us who are in a marriage, strengthen them to die to themselves daily, fully exemplifying unconditional love; and for those who are single, grant us the patience to wait for Your perfect timing as this is the prime time to continually show Your love in ways that would otherwise be more difficult in a marriage. Help us to maximize our time and resources to reach out in love to those in need; and for those of us that are discerning the religious life, may You reveal Your will for our lives so that we can walk forward faithfully, with every crevice in our hearts overwhelming with peace. As Your children that continually seek Your face each and every day, make Your will known and we will follow. In Jesus' perfect name, we pray. Amen!

:)

February 27

Father God, as our beings are composed of body, soul and spirit, You are concerned with all 3. As we anticipate the resurrection of the dead and we are restored our new heavenly bodies, help us to take care of the body You have entrusted to us today. Remove from us this "entitlement" mentality this society faithfully breeds but instill in us a gratitude for the bodies You have blessed us with. Remind us that we are on borrowed time and that our bodies do not belong to us but to You. Bloom in us a genuine appreciation of the body You have given us because each and every body was fearfully and wonderfully made. May we glorify You for Your wonderful creation that was formulated specifically for a mission You have commissioned to us on earth. How that mission plays out may vary but it all boils down to a mission of love: to demonstrate our love for You and for our neighbors. Help us to not fret about what happens in between birth and death but to have full assurance of the resurrection of the dead as we are rejoined with our bodies and enjoy eternity with You. In Jesus' sweet name, we pray. Amen!! :)

What is your relationship with your physical body like? Do you have a healthy relationship or an unhealthy relationship?

February 28

Father God, so easily can we be distracted by the flashy things of this world, all promising happiness and security but never deliver. Surrounded by people in the rat race of the American Dream, we can easily get lost about the true meaning of life and our purpose here on earth. Daily we must recommit our lives, dedicating ourselves to Your work so that we don't lose focus. Lord, help us to slow down, look around and praise You for all that You are. Help us to be grateful for what You have already given us and less focused about what we don't have. Forgive us for when we covet what is our neighbors' rather than praising You for blessing them and seeking wholeness in You. Help us to detach from worldly possessions so that we can be fully devoted to You and the life You have planned for us. Although material blessings are good, they are not the source of true happiness. May we always remember the Hand that provides those blessings to us so that we can be aware that what we have does not truly belong to us but is temporarily entrusted to us to be blessings to others. As we are on the pursuit of happiness, may we remember that true Happiness is actually pursuing us and all we have to do is stop, turn around and embrace Jesus. The person of Jesus Christ will not only make you happy but will fill you to the brim with overwhelming peace, hope and joy- sentiments that is unchanging with the ever changing circumstances.

February 29

Dear God, we were created to bear fruit for your kingdom. May we wake up each morning with the desire to prune away anything that is holding us back so that we can nourish what will bear fruit. May we not be resistant to when You are doing your good work in us but that we will fully embrace it. Create in us a clean heart, O Lord, and renew a steadfast spirit in us. May we be willing to serve you every day of our lives. In Jesus' name, Amen!

What are the fruits in your life that you have been bearing for God's Kingdom? How can you continue to bear more fruit?

March 1

Father God, often times we either live in the
past or live in the future but miss the incredible
gift of today. Help us to be content wherever
we are for our peace and joy lies not in our
circumstances but in who You are. In excess and
in poverty, help us to see the blessings in every
situation. Wealth gives us the opportunity to
share and bless others; poverty gives us the
opportunity to depend on You, waiting to see
miracles happen. No matter where we are in
life, help us not to look around but to keep our
eyes on You as we gaze into the deepness of
Your love. In Jesus' precious name we pray.
Amen! :)

How can you be more content with today? Do
you find yourself in poverty or abundance? How
can that be used for God's glory?

Father God, we thank you for the blessing of work that You grant us the ability to do each and every day. May we rise up in the morning with the fresh desire to partake 100% in the work that has been entrusted to us, knowing full well that it is this work that brings You glory. Revitalize our spirits so that when we work, we work as unto You and not merely for another human being. And may we find joy in doing the work and not feel obligated leading us to count the hours until we can go home again. Rather than doing the minimum at work, may we find the strength to do more than is expected. It is at work that we spend the majority of our day and it is at work that we can share Your light with those around us. May we not miss this opportunity as we anticipate another work day with a lively and excited spirit. We ask that You would energize us once again with the excitement to partake in Your work 24 hours of the day. In Jesus' mighty name, we pray. Amen!!

:)

What is your relationship with work like? Do you put in 100% every day? Can your perspective of work be improved?

March 3

Lord Jesus, thank You for the simplicity of the greatest commandments of the Law: loving God and loving our neighbor with all of our hearts, minds and soul. Though we fail each day to fully love You, the Holy Trinity and our neighbors, we thank You for Your patience in our shortcomings and the new opportunities You grant us each day to love. May we never miss these opportunities but die to ourselves daily so that Your love will be manifest on earth. In Jesus' loving name, we pray. Amen! :)

March 4

Father God, thank you for yet another day where we can wake up and glorify Your name. May we not lose sight of our purpose on earth but keep driven towards the goal of heaven. May we be intentional in all that we do, fully aware that anything and everything will have eternal effects. May no action be too small or insignificant, but fully knowing that You can take something as small as a mustard seed and make it magnificent. Instill in us once again, the joy that radiates through all that we do and becomes contagious to the people around us. And may we never forget the wonderful sacrifice of Your Son, Jesus who took a small act of obedience and gave us the gift of eternal life. In Jesus' mighty name, we pray. Amen!

March 5

Lord Jesus, thank You for being the awesome reward at the end of this marathon race called Life. May we never falter in our journey towards heaven as we make a conscious decision each and every day to follow You in all of Your ways. When the road gets tough, may we fixate our eyes on You as to not get discouraged by the chaos that surrounds us. Help us to be like the wise virgins that prepared ahead of time and brought extra oil fully anticipating Your return. May we not fall asleep to our mission here on earth so that we can encounter You face to face one day in heaven and hear You speak the ever sweet words "Well done, good and faithful servant". In Your beautiful name we pray. Amen! :)

How has your life been like a marathon? Are you prepared to run this race?

March 6

Father God, there is nothing that we can experience here on earth that You cannot say You have not experienced Yourself. Thank You for being so relatable, truly a personal God that wants to get close to our hearts. In times of sorrow and rejection, may we look to Jesus who was countlessly rejected by the very same ones He came to save. Jesus was not exempt from any human emotion but fully experienced the pangs of sorrow and rejection. Our dear Lord and Savior Himself was rejected in His hometown, wept over Jerusalem and mourned for His close friend, Lazarus. Thank You for being the God that You are, one that we can run to and fall into Your arms, knowing that You know exactly what we are going through. In everything, may we give thanks and surrender our lives, the good and the bad. In Jesus' mighty name, we pray. Amen!! :)

What experience are you going through or have gone through that Jesus can relate to directly?

Father God, thank You for being such an exciting and mysterious God. While we have our entire lives to get to know You, we will spend the rest of eternity to get to know You even more! Truly You are inexhaustible and we are blessed to have the opportunity to gaze upon Your awesomeness for all the days of our lives. You reveal just enough to tantalize us but conceal the rest as mysteries that capture our attention. Though we know You are coming back, we do not know exactly when. Like a thief in the night, You instruct us to always be prepared. Lord, may we not fall asleep to the mission You have assigned to each of us, but that we are full of enthusiasm for the work given to us each day. May our hearts blaze in anticipation that today may be the day that our dear Lord and Savior comes back- but even if it's not today, we will continue to do our duties as Your faithful servants. In Jesus' name we pray. Amen!! :)

What mysteries of God intrigue you and keep you on your toes?

March 8

Father God, thank you for not being boring. As the Creator of the universe and the designer of all things beautiful, You like to mix things up a bit. For an immutable and unchanging God, You like to change things in our lives to make it exciting. Whenever we get comfortable somewhere, Your Holy Spirit nudges us to pick up our stuff and move somewhere else. When things get too easy, You nudge us towards opportunities that we are called to take. When life is going smoothly down one road, the path splits into two and major life changing decisions have to be made. But we know that You do this on purpose so that we rely on You every step of the way. We may not see where the road bends, but we know that You can. And as long as we keep our eyes on You, we are sure to be safe. Lord, teach us to have flexible hearts that is not trying to control the steering wheel but rather holding onto Your hand as You direct us through life. And just like You have shown us in the past, when You're in control, the journey may be adventurous but we will get to our destination just fine. May we trust You in all of Your ways. In Jesus' name we pray. Amen! :)

How has God made your life exciting and adventurous? When has He taken you out of your comfort zone and pushed you to greater limits?

March 9

Father God, how unfathomable is Your love for us! You love us so much that You desire that we take part in Your plan of salvation. Though You can easily snap Your divine fingers and grant salvation to everyone, You choose to use us to bring Your love to others. May we take this holy task seriously and be the aroma of Christ to everyone that we meet. Though they may not physically see Christ, they know He's around because He lives in us. And may we be bold and confident in the relationship that we have where it burns deep in our souls not to share. Remind us that we are only responsible for planting the seed but You are the one that grows the seed that was faithfully planted. No doubt, when we team up with our Creator, awesome things happen. No deed or word is too small when it's done with the One who can amplify our efforts 100 fold. May we go forth into our lives looking for opportunities to be that still small light of hope in a hurting world. In Jesus' mighty name we pray. Amen! :)

What small seeds of love have you planted recently? Are there other opportunities that you may have missed?

March 10

Dear God, thank You for creating a life that is so dynamic with its ups and downs, ins and outs, twists and turns. You created things in life that were designed for a proper setting and when taken out of context can be devastating. We know from experience that there is a time and place for everything. There is a time to fast and a time to feast. There is a time to cheer and a time to weep. Lord, in every situation, whatever it may be, may we know the proper action to take to reap the most beauty. When it's time to weep, may we shed some tears with our neighbor; when it's time to cheer, may we raise up a glass and toast to the One who made it all possible. When it's time to change, may we move on with the new but not forget the past. Lord, help us to see the beauty in every situation and praise You through it all. In Jesus' precious name we pray. Amen!! :)

What seasons have you experienced in your life recently? Were they seasons of joy or sorrow? Did you experience them properly?

March 11

Dear God, thank You for being in control. Even when things seem chaotic, You're standing right there watching it all, devising a plan to make it all work out for Your greater glory. When Mary was presented the opportunity to serve You by bearing Jesus in her womb, it certainly was not under ideal conditions. In fact, it was a life-threatening circumstance that You had intentionally placed her in to test her faith. May we all learn from her humble example, trusting in You even when we think You have abandoned us. May we cling ever so tightly when we go through the storms of life, knowing that we will get out even stronger bringing You even MORE glory than if skies were always so beautiful and blue. As the integrity of our character and souls are tested with fire, may we accept the challenge when You lead us into difficult times, with the dim small hope deep in our hearts that You are holding everything in Your hands. In Jesus' powerful name, we pray. Amen!! :)

What difficult time have you experienced lately that You have to entrust to God?

March 12

Father God, thank You for being all-sufficient for us. When we lack, You are the source of grace. We offer up 5 loaves and 2 fish and You feed 5000. It is in our needs that Your miracles and acts of mercy can be seen. May we not seek fulfillment in the world but seek satisfaction in You. Though the ways of the world say otherwise, complete joy and peace can be attained simply by running to You. When chaos surrounds us and nothing is going right, deep peace can resound in our hearts, assuring us that everything will be okay. In little, may our hearts be filled with gratitude as You provide with Your miraculous hands. In much, may we be that vessel that You use to provide for those that are in need. As one family, we meet each other's needs - forming the Body of Christ. May You always be all that we need. In Jesus' name we pray. Amen! :)

How has God provided when you were in need? Have you been able to be satisfied with all that God provided for you?

Father God, thank you for establishing Your
Church here on earth to guide us to Your love.
Any good shepherd would not leave his sheep
unattended but taken care of. This Church,
though not perfect, is intended to lead, teach
and equip us with the tools it takes to live a
life that glorifies You. Through Your direct
instruction, You taught us to forgive and pray
for those who have hurt us. You have taught us
to love those who do evil, assuring us that love
conquers all. You have shown us what humility
looks like so that we can walk in Your footsteps.
And Your example did not stop impacting Your
people from 2000 years ago but still impacts us
today. You have entrusted Your people to the
Church and we pray that the Church leaders
will continually uphold their responsibility with
utmost regard. Lord, please continue to build
Your Church which is faithfully working to bring
Your kingdom here on earth, as it is in heaven.
In Your precious name we pray. Amen! :)

How has the Church been a blessing of guidance
in your life? Have you been praying for our
Church leaders recently?

March 14

Father God, thank You for deeming our hearts worthy of Your presence. If You truly reside in our hearts, then out of the overflow of our hearts pour out Your goodness and mercy. Help us not to criticize our neighbors but lift them up. Show us the good in people so that we can strengthen those attributes while the vices shrivel up and weaken. May we be mirrors of Your love so that when people encounter us they can see that they too are a reflection of who You are. Show us that each person bears Your image and thus are truly valuable in Your eyes. There is no life, whether unborn, born or passed on to eternity that didn't matter but bears much significance, even if the individual or society as a whole believes it or not. May our hearts be overflowing with Your love that it cannot be contained within the confines of ourselves but becomes active to fight darkness and brighten up the world, one heart at a time. In Jesus' mighty name we pray. Amen! :)

Do you believe that your heart is worthy of His presence? Do you reflect His love to others and lift them up? Do you see God in every person you meet?

Father God, though there is no contradiction in You, You love the "counter intuitive" economy. In order for us to save our lives, we must lose it for Your sake. We must love not only our friends but our enemies. In Your kingdom, the first is last and the last is first. We must be like children to enter the kingdom of heaven. Blessed are the poor in spirit for theirs is the kingdom of heaven. You, God, saw it fit to come down to earth as a feeble infant born into a poor family. You were born in a manger and rode a donkey, instead of a palace and horse suited for a King. Lastly, You decided that our Creator will die on the cross at the hands of the Created- yet our Lord forgives them for they do not know what they are doing. Lord, may we embrace Your perfect example and implement it into our lives so that we can be more like You.

Grant us the ability to understand this "counter- intuitive" economy of Your kingdom. To be able to sing psalms while persecuted in prison. To stop and pray when chaos abounds all around. For strong men to fall on their knees in order to stand strong in the face of opposition. For us to die to ourselves in order to really live.

In everything, may we see our reality with spiritual eyes. In Jesus' name we pray. Amen! :)

What is your understanding of God's counter-intuitive economy? Do you struggle with the way God likes to work in our lives?

Father God, thank You for showing us rather than telling us. It is often easier said than done, so You decided that it was best to show us how it's done. The path to holiness is not an easy path, but one that requires constant self-denial. While our selfish desires push us to strive for number one, You tell us that the first will be last and the last will be first. As society drives us to have the latest and best gadget, You tell us to humble ourselves and be content with what we have. As we seek to climb the social ladder, You came down from heaven not to be served but to serve and give Your life as a ransom for many. Living in a world that continually contradicts the Mandates of Heaven, we have to actively orient our gaze heavenward, following in the footsteps of Your Son who has successfully shown the way. Lord, grant us the ability to live in this world but not of this world, as our citizenship is that of Heaven. In Jesus' name we pray. Amen! :)

Do you tend to tell people or show people how to live? How can we show people more than telling?

March 17

Father God, thank You for celebratory times. As King Solomon once wrote, there is a time for sorrow and a time for joy- and with each appropriate time, we should act accordingly. Celebratory times demonstrate that life is truly a roller coaster of a journey and there indeed are times of joy in this ride. Celebratory times help us to gather together and build the bonds of friendship. Celebratory times give us the fuel and motivation we need to get through the tough times when we encounter them, knowing full well another time of celebration is just around the corner. Lord, may we embrace the celebratory times in our lives and fully indulge in them, knowing that they are blessings being bestowed upon us from You. In Your precious name we pray. Amen! :)

What times of celebration have been a blessing to you? How have they been helpful to endure moments of difficulty?

March 18

Father God, thank You for being all sufficient for us. Help us to shift our focus from us to You and all Your love and goodness. When life seems unfair, may we not dwell on that but run to the cross and unload our cares and concerns there. May we look at everything in our lives with Your perspective where things just fade away in comparison to Your love. We ask that You strengthen us in times of temptation where in each opportunity we are stronger when we overcome and forgive ourselves when we fall. Lord, in times of trials, may we feel Your presence and burrow our faces into Your bosom so that we can be comforted by Your warmth and heartbeat. In Jesus' mighty name, we pray. Amen!! :)

Have you ever felt that life was unfair? Does that matter in comparison to God's love and provision for us? Life may be unfair but it's still beautiful...

March 19

Dear God, thank You for showing us that pride is the root of all vice and humility is the root of all virtue. Humility is not thinking less of ourselves but thinking of ourselves less. Our hearts naturally tend to be selfish and place oneself first; but teach us to humble ourselves and put others before us. Before trying to meet our needs, help us to serve others. In Your counter-intuitive economy, the first is last and the last is first. It is when we fully embrace this concept that we realize that our true fulfillment is found in You and not our position. Thank You for Your example of coming down from heaven not to be served but to serve and to give Your life as a ransom for us. May we find our satisfaction not in our stature or circumstances but in the unshakable truth of You. Today we ask for strength as we exercise our "humility" muscle to strengthen our virtues so that we can be more and more like You. In Jesus' strong name we pray. Amen!! :)

How can we practice the virtue of humility today? How can we serve others more than we serve ourselves?

March 20

Dear God, thank You for sending Your Son to teach us here on earth. Because of our limited and finite minds, You saw it fit to incarnate Yourself to show us face-to-face how to love. Though we tend to resort to our prideful tendencies, teach us to be humble ourselves enough to listen and accept Your ways. Soften our hearts so that we can be teachable and mold our hearts in the shape it needs to be in order to completely follow You. Help us not to be stubborn or rigid in our ways where we can easily miss the beauty of the truth. Though You taught in parables, grant us spiritual eyes to see the spiritual truth of Your reality. In everything, Lord, may we see You as the Great Teacher showing us how to be better in step with the guidance of the Holy Spirit. And when we don't understand all the details, grant us humble hearts to trust Your guidance. In Jesus' sweet name we pray. Amen! :)

How has Jesus' earthly mission helped you better understand His Truth and way of life?

Dear God, thank You for the ability to practice self- discipline. Though we are inclined to be selfish, we can choose daily to die to ourselves and put others before us. Help us not to let jealousy or selfish ambition to prevent us from seeking the good of others. When someone succeeds, may we have genuine joy for that person in their accomplishment. When someone is being used for the advancement of the Kingdom, may we praise You for using that person instrumentally for Your greater glory. When someone is blessed with a gift or ability, may we work with them synergistically to produce even greater results. Lord, teach us to work as one and to function as Your hands and feet. May we take on a lowly servant position to be great in Your eyes. Create in us a pure and satisfied heart, grateful for all that You have blessed us with, as well as our neighbors. In Jesus' complete name we pray. Amen!! :)

How have you worked synergistically with another person's gifts and talents for a greater purpose?

March 22

Father God, thank You for understanding our feeble hearts. Though we have everything we need to believe, we still fall into moments of doubt. When faced with yet another mountain, we question Your ability to help us climb over. When another storm sweeps over our path, we doubt that the sun is still shining above the clouds. Though Your Son has demonstrated incredible miracles to provide credibility to His claims, we still doubt His identity as our Lord and Savior. God, we believe but we ask that You would help us with our unbelief. Help us to believe Your promises even though they may seem impossible. Help us to believe that You love us and that You are mindful of us even though we may feel insignificant and unimportant. Lord, grant us not only knowledge of You and all Your promises but faith in order for them to come alive in our hearts. In Jesus' mighty name, we pray. Amen! :)

What doubts have you experienced lately?

Father God, thank You for being our friend. And
not just any friend but a GOOD friend at that.
Even when we fail, You patiently wait for us to
come around. Sometimes it takes days, months
and even years for us to realize our faults,
swallow our pride and restore our relationship
with You. Lord, help us to invest in the
friendship we have with You, making time in our
busy schedules to spend quality time with You,
conversing with You throughout the day, sharing
with You our fears and dreams, our sorrows and
our joys. We can be as real and raw as any
friendship can be because You love us to the
very thread of our being. Lord, may we model
the kind of friend You are to us in our other
earthly friendships, sharing the love You have
for us with others so that they too may come to
know You. As with any good thing, may we not
keep our friendship with You a secret but
something we proudly wear on our sleeves. In
Jesus' awesome name we pray. Amen! :)

How has God been a good friend to you?

March 24

Dear God, thank You for the gift of wisdom in our lives. Wisdom is the ability to think and act using knowledge, understanding, common sense and insight. A prudent person sees trouble down the road and will take action to avoid the trouble; however, a fool will also see trouble down the road but continues on his way. Lord, thank You for our elders and people who have come before us and know much about the road. May we humble ourselves to accept the advice and wisdom our elders wish to bestow upon us. While the world around us proclaim that we should "live and learn", You wish for us to "learn and live" so that we do not make the same mistakes others have done. Along those same lines, may we learn from the wisdom of the Saints who have treaded this path before and have succeeded in the journey to heaven. May we surround ourselves with people of wisdom, both alive on earth and alive in heaven so that we are better equipped to tackle this life for God's glory. In Jesus' mighty name, we pray. Amen!! :)

How has wisdom played in your life? Would you say you have been very prudent thus far?

"The beginning of wisdom is this: Get wisdom. Though it cost all you have, get understanding." -Proverbs 4:7

Father God, thank You for a future. While we look back and thank You, we look around and serve You, we look ahead and trust You. As St. Augustine would like to say, though every Saint has a past, every sinner has a future. While we set on to do Your work, may we not look back on what we have left behind, good or bad, but keep our eyes on the road ahead of us so that the plow of our lives remains straight. A disciple that looks back is not fit for the Kingdom, so help us to keep our gaze fixed on the road ahead. As long as our eyes are set on You, we can be sure to stay afloat in the sea of life, steadily pushing forward toward the goal of heaven. No matter what has happened in our past, we can be certain that the future is promising if we walk with You. As we set out to live for You, whether it be the religious or married life, may we detach ourselves from the world so that our joy and satisfaction is rooted in You and nothing but You. In Jesus' mighty name, we pray. Amen! :)

Have you been able to focus on your future and keeping your past in the past?

March 26

Father God, thank You for making us 1 being with 3 components. We are not only body, soul or spirit but ALL three at the same time. Though we are essentially spirits, we are enfleshed to be able to operate in the material realm. Though we are fleshy beings, we have emotional and intellectual capabilities that define our personalities. Though we are physically and emotionally capable, we are also spiritually inclined, with the capability of connecting our spirits with Your Holy Spirit that guides and directs us towards the path of holiness. It is only when we are mindful of all 3 components and exercise those parts of our being that we can reach our full potential. May we not diminish our existence to simply the physical, emotional or spiritual realm but fully embrace all 3 characteristics of our being. As we were created to be eternal and spend eternity with You, we ask that You would grant salvation to those who express indifference or who have completely rejected Your love. We implore you to soften their hearts and bring them back to Your fold. In Jesus' name we pray. Amen!! :)

What is your relationship with all 3 components of our being? Do you acknowledge all 3?

March 27

Dear God, thank You for creating us as emotional beings, with the ability to fully experience all that life has to offer. It's not enough to be intellectually and physically aware of the world around us but emotionally connected so that the experience of life is all that more interesting. We not only feel the wind blow through our hair, but also Your arms wrap around our heart. You gave us the gift of emotions so that we can get to know You better and to express how You feel towards us. As beautiful as emotions can be in our lives, if left unchecked, they can get out of hand and even become detrimental to us. Lord, grant us the strength to surrender our emotions to You and allow You to mold it in such a way that brings You glory. In Jesus' mighty name, we pray. Amen! :)

Have your emotions been a blessing in your life or a detriment? We must be able to have a good, healthy relationship with our emotions.

March 28

Father God, thank You for placing eternity in our hearts. Simply taking a look around us shows us that this world is temporal and we were made for eternity. Though things of this world are important, may they not distract us from the real important matters of the spirit. May our spirit be undisturbed when chaos surrounds us. When the winds blow in every direction, may our hearts be steadied by the anchor of Your Love. When life gets crazy, may we cling ever so tightly to You- understanding that nothing is as important as our walk with You. May we use every opportunity to surrender our will and bring You glory. In Jesus' name we pray. Amen!
:)

"He has made everything beautiful in its time. He has also set eternity in the human heart; yet no one can fathom what God has done from beginning to end." -Ecclesiastes 3:11

March 29

Dear God, thank You for all the blessings You bestow upon us each and every day. Forgive us when we rush past the rose bush that You allowed to grow for our enjoyment. Forgive us when we focus on everything that is going wrong and not on what's going right. Forgive us when complaints are upon our tongues rather than praises that fill our lungs. Lord, grant us hearts that are aware of the continuous blessings that surround us on a daily basis and teach us to surrender to You whatever that may be weighing down on our hearts. In Jesus' mighty name we pray. Amen! :)

March 30

Father God, thank You for being worth it. You are that precious jewel we find and desire to sell all our possessions to have it. You are that everlasting living water that satisfies our souls and makes all the fresh and crisp water of the world stale in comparison. You alone are enough to sacrifice our selfish desires and die to ourselves on a daily basis so that we can obtain life in You. When life seems to become tough and bland, may we shift our gaze towards You and realize that You are worth it all. In Jesus' name we pray. Amen!! :)

March 31

Dear God, thank You for showing us what it means to be generous. You truly love a cheerful giver because it is not about WHAT we give but about HOW we give. The condition of our heart enables us to happily part with anything that we truly value. Show us that true wealth is not about what we keep but about what we give away. May we be generous with our time, talent and treasure knowing full well that You see our every effort to serve our neighbor and may You grant that our wealth is multiplied in heaven. In Jesus' name, we pray. Amen! :)

What is your attitude about giving to others?
Do you give with a cheerful heart?

"Each of you should give what you have decided in your heart to give, not reluctantly or under compulsion, for God loves a cheerful giver." 2 Corinthians 9:7

April 1

Father God, thank You for creating us with the desire to work. When You made Adam and Eve, You told them to subdue the earth and have dominion over every living creature. When Jesus came down to earth, He came with a mission in mind. Every saint that has gone before us has lived their life with mission and purpose, never shying away from any hard work that was presented to them. May we live with that same intention in our hearts, willing to do our best in every opportunity that comes our way. May we find meaning in the work that we commit to do during our life and never forget the real meaning of our being. May we not get caught up with the details of our work but to see the bigger picture of how everything fits into the grand scheme of things. In every area of our work, the easy, the mundane and the challenging, may we bring our attention back to You and ultimately bring You glory with our lives. As nothing that is worth pursuing comes easy, grant us strength to keep pushing forward when the going gets rough, keeping our eyes on the prize. In Jesus' name we pray. Amen! :)

What is your relationship with work like?

April 2

Dear God, thank You for being the "great maestro". You are the one that is conducting all the little details of our lives, making sure everything comes together to make something beautiful. Like a grand orchestra, we play only one part of the big picture but You are aware of everything that is happening. Though we are unaware of what the future holds, may we sit back and relax, knowing full well that You have everything under control. When things seem chaotic, bring to our attention the reality that You can make everything work out for our good. Truly, some of the greatest blessings are when things happen unexpectedly. Lord, may we entrust to You everything that You have entrusted to us- our lives, our families, our work, our possessions, our friends and relationships. There is nothing that we have that You didn't give to us. May we regard everything as blessings granted to us on borrowed time and surrender them to You because they are Yours to begin with. In Jesus' mighty name, we pray. Amen! :)

How has God worked as the "great maestro" in your life?

April 3

Father God, thank You for new beginnings. As each day is a new day, full of possibilities, may we rise up from our beds refreshed leaving behind everything from the days before and anticipating the days ahead. Though we may continually slip and fall, we will continually rise up again ready to take the next step forward. Though we make mistakes and hurt our neighbor unintentionally, we can rectify our blunders and move forward. Though the past is full of accomplishments and failures, may we not get discouraged but rely on You all the more. May we focus on how far we've come and not on how far we have to go. May we focus on our success and not our failures. May we keep our eyes on You and not the circumstances that surround us. In everything, Lord, make all things new again so that we can start afresh. In Jesus' name we pray. Amen! :)

How do you approach the new day? Do you tend to carry the weight of yesterday or do you start afresh?

April 4

Dear God, thank you for being a God of Wisdom. As we are created in Your image, we bear the essence of wisdom in our lives. As Your Holy Spirit guides us down the path of righteousness, we can be assured that we are growing in wisdom. Wisdom is not necessarily the accumulation of knowledge but fruitful synthesis from that knowledge that manifests itself is various ways. It's the ability to filter through junk information that would contaminate our souls and seek that which would enhance our walk. Wisdom is not something that is bought or easily attained but a virtue that is exercised and practiced through the journey of life. It's not a one-time thing but a process. Lord, grant us the strength to continue to seek Your face in all that we do as we grow in wisdom. In Jesus' name we pray. Amen!! :)

How have you been growing in wisdom throughout your life?

April 5

Father God, thank You for the gift of hope. When everything around us seem dismal, may we fixate our eyes on that small glimmer of light. When people around us tell us to quiet down, may we shout all the more to Jesus, knowing full well that all blessings come from Him. When things get difficult, may we focus on the potential for everything to clear up. In every storm, though it may seem long and drawn out, there is an end to the wind and the rain. May we understand that we are human and You are God. We do our part waiting faithfully for You to do Your part. In everything, help us to do our best and leave the rest to You. In Jesus' name we pray. Amen! :)

What is your attitude like when you go through storms? Are you hopeful that it will soon pass or do you wallow around in misery? How can we develop better responses to storms in our lives?

"May the God of hope fill you with all joy and peace as you trust in him, so that you may overflow with hope by the power of the Holy Spirit." -Romans 15:13

April 6

Father God, thank You for the power of multiplication. Although with just our abilities, we cannot go far, You like to take the little that we have and stretch it further than we could ever imagine. We offer You our mustard seed and You make it grow into a tree. We offer You 5 loaves and 2 fish and You feed 5,000. We offer You our 2 pennies and You build a ministry out of it. We offer You the purity and faithfulness of our words and You can use it to save a life. Lord, may we never underestimate what You could do with the little that we have but that we remain faithful to do our part and entrusting that You are taking care of the rest. In Jesus' mighty name, we pray. Amen! :)

Do you believe that God can take the little that you have to offer and multiply it? How does that change the way you can impact the world?

April 7

Dear God, thank You for the ability to give. When we give, we realize that we have more than we need and that we can share out of the surplus that we have. When we give, we trust You to provide and not hoard onto things that we may need later. When we give, our hearts open up to love in ways that would be otherwise impossible. When we give, our generosity meets the needs of our neighbors and enables them to grow stronger in their walk. When we give in our tithes and offerings, we realize that You really don't need the treasures that we lift up but it is us that benefit from this practice that You instruct us to do. For when we give, our focus is re-oriented from petty worries and concerns of this world and back to what's really important and what really matters. We ask that today You would mold our hearts in such a way that is willing to be generous with what has been entrusted to us. In Jesus' name we pray, amen! :)

How has giving to others been a blessing to you?

April 8

Dear God, thank You for the gift of eternity. With an eternal perspective in mind, the petty details of this life fade away. Situations requiring forgiveness becomes clear when we realize this life is short and we have to prepare for eternity. Situations of frustration become silly when we understand that it doesn't really matter in the grand scheme of things. Situations of materialism become trivial when we foresee that all things turn to dust. Situations of trials becomes joy when we realize that we are deemed worthy to suffer for Your Name's sake, sanctifying our souls and walking closer to You. With eternity in mind, everything focuses into perspective and at the end of our earthly journey, our lives glorify You. Lord, grant us an eternal perspective in all that we do so that we can surrender everything and walk in freedom. In Jesus' name we pray. Amen! :)

How has the view of eternity impacted the way you live your life?

April 9

Dear God, thank You for the gift of time. While You are eternal with no beginning and no end, we are finite beings that live in real time. With eternity in mind, may we choose to live this life in light of our everlasting destiny. But while here on earth, we observe the rule of the sun rising and setting, the days rolling by and calendar weeks, months and years constantly changing. May we never take one day for granted but understand that everything is temporal and will one day come to an end. Until then, grant us the strength to keep our eyes on the goal so that we can resist temptation when it comes our way. In Jesus' name we pray.

Amen! :)

What is your view on time? Do you find yourself thinking you have a lot of time and tend to squander it? Or are you aware that your days are numbered and try to make the best of every moment?

April 10

Father God, thank You for the gift of individuality. While we are meant to be in community, we are not called to be so caught up in other people's lives. Although we influence each other, help each other along the way, we should not dwell on each other. As You have granted each and every one of us unique gifts and talents, may we not desire what is our neighbors', but rather thanking You for the different blessings You have bestowed upon them and ourselves. May we not focus on the sin that our neighbor may be harboring, but gently and surely show them the log in their eye.

When we stand before Your throne on judgement day, it is not the virtues and vices that our neighbors have that You look at but the virtues and vices that we have cultivated in our own lives. In every day, may we be faithful with the gifts and talents that You have entrusted to us, bringing You glory with our lives no matter the circumstances that are presented to us. In Jesus' name, we pray. Amen!

:)

What is your relationship like with others in your community? Are you able to be part of others' lives but not consumed by them?

April 11

Dear God, thank You for the graces that You shower in our lives. You not only show us mercy by not giving us what we deserve, but You also bless us with Your grace, giving us what we don't deserve. With Your grace, we muster up the strength to resist temptation and live righteous lives. Being a God with infinite amount of grace, we ask that You would be generous in blessing us with Your graces so that we can continue to live lives that glorify You. In Jesus' mighty name, we pray. Amen! :)

April 12

Father God, thank You for being the stream of living water that gives us life when we are thirsty. As Psalm 1 points out, the individual who adheres to Your law and meditates on it day and night is someone who is planted by the streams of water that yields its fruit in due time. Just as we cannot rush a fruit to grow, we cannot rush the fruits in our own lives to grow. The leaves of the tree planted by streams of water will never wither or fade despite the storms that pass by. And all that the tree sets out to do will be successful, bearing fruit in the right season. Father, help us not to grow weary when we don't see the fruit grow as fast as we would like it to grow. Grant us patience as we wait upon Your perfect timing. In Jesus' mighty name, we pray. Amen! :)

April 13

Dear God, thank You for never leaving our side. Often times we shrink from the idea of greatness because we don't think we have what it takes. We may be inadequate as mere humans but God is not and He wants to mold you into something magnificent. With the little that we have, whether it be time, talent or treasure, may we offer it up to God so that He can make something substantial out of it. Holiness may be unattainable on our own accord, but God calls each and every one of us to become saints and He equips us with what it takes to accomplish such task. Though we may be finite, we serve a God who is infinite and nothing is impossible for God. Today may we not underestimate the abilities of our God and keep our eyes on the goal of greatness. In Jesus' name we pray, amen! :)

April 14

Father God, thank You for giving us the spirit of peace and not fear. In times that we are fearful, we can be certain that that spirit does not come from You and we can rebuke it. You never promised us that we would never go through tough times but that You would be there with us as we walk through the valley of death together. It is during these times of fire that we are purified and perfected. May we not look for difficulty but embrace the opportunities You provide us so that we can be sanctified and look more like You. In Jesus' powerful name we pray. Amen! :)

Father God, thank You for giving us the gift of faith. Faith enables us to believe that with You, all things are possible. Faith gives us hope in the dreariest of times. That glimmer of hope that grants us the strength to keep pushing forward when everything seems so bleak. But our faith is not blind. In fact, our faith is evidence-based faith. You are a God that provides us with proof of Your existence with just a glance at the creation around us. You assure us of Your presence by the peace and comfort You give us even while going through a storm. You performed miracles to validate the claims that You made through Jesus. You command us to remember the exodus of Passover and other remarkable events of history to remind our feeble human minds of the magnificent God that we serve. Our awesome God can't be contained in a box and requires us to have faith that He is taking care of us, because He always has. May we trust that God has everything under control and that we exercise the gift of our evidence-based faith. In Jesus' mighty name, amen! :)

What is your faith like? Is it more blind faith or evidence-based?

"He replied, 'If you have faith as small as a mustard seed, you can say to this mulberry tree, 'Be uprooted and planted in the sea,' and it will obey you." – Luke 17:6

April 16

Father God, thank You for the gift of prayer. In this sacred form of communication, we can remain connected to You, our source of life. It is through prayer that we can praise You for the wondrous deeds You do in our lives. It is through prayer that we can request divine help in our daily struggles. It is through prayer that we come together with all the angels and the saints to glorify Your name. In this busy and hectic life, may we diligently set aside time in our schedules to get refueled and spend quality time with our Creator. In Jesus' name we pray. Amen!

:)

April 17

Dear God, thank You for giving us the Holy Spirit. At our baptism, we were not just baptized with water, which has no power to create change, but with the Holy Spirit. It is through the Holy Spirit that we are granted the power to become holy as our Father in Heaven is holy. It is through the Holy Spirit that we can strive and become saints as we are all called to be. It is through the Holy Spirit that we can radiate God's love, mercy and peace to those around us, meeting each other's needs as they are presented to us. May we not take the gift of the Holy Spirit for granted and exercise this wonderful treasure that resides in our hearts to create holiness that would be otherwise impossible. In Jesus' precious name, we pray. Amen! :)

April 18

God, thank You for the gift of You. We love You not for what You do for us or what You give us but because You are our loving Heavenly Father. In times when our prayers seem to be falling on deaf ears and nothing seems to be going right, we know that You are standing right by our side feeling our pain. You want to bless us with abundance and prosperity but we have to be patient, trusting in Your perfect design. Help us not to love You for the gifts that You give us but rather love You because You are our Creator and You are all that we need. In Jesus' sweet name we pray. Amen! :)

April 19

Dear God, thank You for being our joy. In a society where our happiness seems to be dependent on external circumstances such as our job, our house, our car etc. You tell us that our joy transcends the superficial. Since our identity is rooted in You as a son/daughter of the King, and we harbor the gifts of the Holy Spirit, no matter what our situation may be, we can still exhibit complete joy that radiates and gives testimony to the world. Lord, grant us the strength to find the joy deep in our hearts that is stable and consistent, not changing with the changing times. In Jesus' sweet name, we pray. Amen! :)

Do you find yourself joyful no matter the circumstances?

Father God, may we never underestimate the amazing things You can do with the seeds we plant. We may not feel that our part in anything is significant but when we tag team with You, You water the seeds we faithfully plant with heavenly water that gives life to the seed that will grow and produce fruit that is 100 fold. With all of our time, talent and treasure may we eagerly and generously sow the seeds You have given us so that others can grow and benefit. Give us the eyes to see these opportunities so that we are not caught up with trivial "urgent" matters of the world but so that we prioritize matters of the kingdom. Thank You for choosing us to be ambassadors of Your love and grace to the world. May we continue to represent You to the best of our abilities, loving each and every person we encounter. In Jesus' mighty name, we pray. Amen!

Do you recognize the potential of each and every action you do? How can that encourage you to continue to do the small things even though there are "pressing and urgent" matters in your life?

April 21

Father God, thank You for the resurrection. Though we know that You are the God of the living and not the dead, we tend to forget and believe that this life is all there is. We get into this "earthly" mode, storing all our treasure here and not focusing on storing our riches in heaven. We tend to avenge for justice here and forget that justice will eventually be served in heaven. We get so caught up in the little details of life, and forget that it's the big details that matter and warrant our focus while here on earth. We wail in distress when a loved one is taken away but forget that we will once again reunite in heaven. We cry out in anger when death knocks on our door, but we forget that You died, resurrected and conquered death 2000 years ago, and death will be no more. May we dwell on this future grace and be comforted that You have granted us new life in the age to come, that is better than we can ever imagine. In Your name we pray. Amen! :)

What is your relationship with death in this life? Are you tormented at the thought of death or are you comforted with the fact that death is not the end?

Father God, thank You for new beginnings. Just like the morning is the dawn of a new day, with every confession, You grant us a new start. On this path towards holiness, we are expected to trip and fall but by your grace and mercy, You bless us with Your forgiveness. With Your forgiveness we are able to push forward in life towards sanctification, to look more like You with each passing day. The goal in life is heaven and our mission is our vocation. May we not get distracted or confused but keep our eyes up ahead on the prize. With all the forces at work in our lives, may we not become complacent or stagnant in our spiritual life as that will only make us slip further away from You- but rather instill in us a desire to run with full force towards You as You create saints in us. In Jesus' awesome name we pray. Amen! :)

How has confession freed you from a sin that you committed and allowed you to move forward? Does the priest remind you of Jesus who would say "Go and sin no more"?

April 23

Dear Jesus, thank You for being the truth of life. Constantly being bombarded with lies can drag us and make us downtrodden. But when we wake up with the decision to rebuke the lies and cling ever so closely to You, those lies start to get drowned out while the still whispers of Your truth become louder. The only way to know Your promises is to inundate ourselves in Your good Word- keeping all that You say at the forefront of our minds and slowly starving off the lies.

While the lies of the evil one bind us, Your truth sets us free. While the schemes of the evil one are designed to steal, kill and destroy, Your promises are beautifully designed to bring life and bring it more abundantly. May we be reminded of our identities as sons and daughters of the Most High King and cling to the truth of Your promises which brings life and sets us free. In Jesus' powerful name we pray. Amen! :)

April 24

Father God, thank You for giving us the concept of "time". King Solomon tells us that there is a time for everything. A time for life and a time for death. A time for celebration and a time for tears. A time for rest and a time for work. Father God, You make everything beautiful in its right timing and context. May we not strip away the beauty of Your gifts to us by rushing or taking it out of context but enjoy everything in Your perfect time- the way You had intended it to be. In Jesus' name we pray. Amen! :)

Father God, thank You for the gift of repentance. It is when we acknowledge the err in our ways that we can stop, turn around and start to head in Your direction. It's an exercise of humility to admit that we have been wrong the entire time and we submit our will to Yours. It doesn't matter how fast we are going in life; if we're going in the wrong direction, we will ultimately end nowhere. But rather, we self-reflect daily to assess if what we are doing today will take us where we want to be tomorrow. Lord, we want to be with You not only for tomorrow but for eternity. May we take this day and every day to recommit our lives to You, repenting in areas that need repentance and take steps towards You and Your fold. In Jesus' precious name we pray. Amen! :)

How quick are you to repent when you realize that you've been wrong? Are you able to stop, turn around and go in the right direction?

April 26

Father God, thank You for the gift of faith. Faith is the divine belief in the unseen. It fills the gap that merges present reality and the anticipated reality. It's the substance that makes the world around us as we know it make sense. It's the belief that everything will work out when the tables could turn either way. It's not enough to just believe it but to act on it.

Belief in You, a Holy and righteous God will make us live like we truly do, for faith without works is dead. Today, may we act in faith for our hopes, dreams and desires, believing that You will meet us half way. In Jesus' powerful name we pray. Amen! :)

How does faith play in your life? Do you tend to have faith that things will work out even if your current circumstance seem grim?

April 27

Father God, thank You for our hearts of worship and praise. Our hearts were created for the very purpose of praising and worshipping You, where our heart is satisfied to its fullest extent. It is no surprise that people often find themselves worshipping other mediums such as work, sports, vanity, celebrities and money when their hearts are not fully worshipping You. Often times, people have displaced You on the throne of their lives and replaced You with themselves. In a culture where narcissism is encouraged and it's all about us, it's easy to get distracted from what satisfies our hearts the most and settle for what's second best. Lord, claim back what is Yours and fill our hearts with Your divine Spirit once again to dwell and reign forever. May we not lose focus of Who we ought to praise and worship so that we are truly satisfied to our little hearts' content. In Jesus' awesome name we pray. Amen! :)

Is God in His rightful place in your heart or is the throne replaced with something/someone else? How can you bring God back to His rightful throne?

Father God, thank You for the obstacles that You place in our lives. Anything that is worth pursuing is not necessarily easy to obtain and You very well know that we need to work for something for it to have any meaning in our lives. As the gate to righteousness is narrow and difficult, we must take up our cross each day, surrender our will to Yours and give it our best- for it is our best that You are looking for. The path of sanctification is not an easy path but it is sure a worthwhile path that will bless us with an eternity of You. Rather than devising schemes to avoid these obstacles that You divinely place in our lives, may we embrace them as opportunities to exercise the Holy Spirit in our hearts as we work with Him as our Paraclete, our helper and advocate. In Jesus' mighty name we pray. Amen! :)

What obstacles have you faced recently? Did they help you to grow?

Father God, thank You making us little light bearers. As little moons that reflect the goodness and light of the sun, we reflect the goodness and light of Your Son. When we are deceived by the lie that we cannot make a difference in this world, we take a look at amazing saints that have gone before us who exemplify the beauty of following You and the impact they had in the world around them. Although we cannot make a difference on our own accord, it is Your Spirit that works in and through us, driving us to team up to be the hands and feet of Christ. Lord, help us to not hold back in sharing the light that we receive from You so that others may see You in us as we light up the world together. In Jesus' awesome name we pray. Amen! :)

How have you been reflecting God's light lately? Do you believe that your little light can help light up the world from all of its darkness?

Dear God, thank You for being the merciful, yet just judge that You are. Though we don't deserve it, You lavish us with Your forgiveness for the sins that we commit. You bestow mercy upon us, not giving us what we deserve and granting us Your grace, blessings that we don't deserve. Although we are forgiven, we must be cognizant of the fact that we still have to face the consequences of our sins. The sin of adultery can be forgiven but the trust has to be built back up again and the wounds have to heal. And when the wounds do heal- it'll never be as it was before, harnessing the past in a scar for all the world to see. But may the scars be a testimony of a repentant heart that has turned away from its crooked ways and committed to walking in holiness. Lord, turn our sins into life and turn our ashes into something beautiful. In Jesus' merciful name we pray. Amen! :)

What sin have you committed that you were forgiven of but still had to face the consequences?

May 1

Father God, thank You for the gift of wisdom and prudence. With so many evil forces at work to kill, steal and destroy us, we must be ready to enter into battle the second our feet touch the ground. All throughout the night, the enemy is whispering lies into our ears wanting to cause dissension and chaos among God's children. Although we interact with other human beings in the physical realm, we must be aware that our fight is not against flesh and blood but against the evil spirits that lurk around us. Instead of fighting our dear neighbors, we should show compassion and rebuke the evil force behind the scenes. Lord, grant us the wisdom and strength to realize that we are all in this together and that the real enemy is not our brother, sister, mother or father but the evil one that seeks our destruction. May we walk around with spiritual eyes that can see the real battle at hand. In Jesus' powerful and mighty name, we pray. Amen! :)

What lies have you been fed to cause dissension between you and your neighbor? How have you overcome those lies?

May 2

Father God, thank You for sending Your Son to show us how to love. Jesus exemplified perfectly what it means to love. Love is not just a feeling but it's an action, a decision, a sacrifice of one's own will. Love endures all things, the good and the bad. We claim to want to be Christ-like, but we don't want the cross. We want to follow Christ but we don't want the rejection. We say that we will stick it to the end but we refuse to die to ourselves and our selfish desires. Jesus showed us dramatically what it means to love completely and totally, even to the cross. Contrary to popular culture, love at times can be very inconvenient but it is only during the tough times that love is perfected. May we look for ways today that we can love our neighbor with our whole selves- looking to Christ for the strength when it gets too hard. In Jesus' powerful name, we pray. Amen! :)

How has your love towards others been sacrificial and inconvenient?

May 3

Father God, thank You for discernment. There will be many instances in life that try our patience and push our buttons but it's up to us to allow something to get us to respond in any which way. On a daily basis, we are presented with situations that can be major or minor, and with the guidance of the Holy Spirit, may we choose our battles wisely, focusing our energies in areas that need our attention and dismissing any situation that is not a big deal at the end of the day. Our daily decisions reflect how our lives will unfold, totally consumed with minor details or calm and collected, saving the energy for when it's needed most. We must remember that the goal is heaven- everything else are just distractions. Lord, grant us the wisdom and strength to determine what battles to fight that will ultimately help us win the war. In Your precious name we pray. Amen! :)

How have you discerned which battles to fight lately? Which battles have you determined to be just distractions and not worth your time, attention and effort?

May 4

Father God, thank You for the gift of prioritization. This world is full of distractions and often times we fall into the trap of doing too much. We understand that many things are considered "good" to do but too much of anything is actually bad. Doing too much is overwhelming and unbearable. In today's day and age, the art of saying "no" needs to be exercised because it is what will ultimately liberate us from the tyranny of the urgent. We need to learn how to give up the good to get what's best. We need to learn how to sacrifice the pawn soldier to win the chess game. We need to say "no" to an unnecessary battle in order to win the war. Contrary to popular culture, less is more - especially when it's surrendered into Your Hands. Lord, today grant us the strength to say "no" to unnecessary activities and distractions in order to commit the time to what's more important. In Jesus' sweet name, we pray. Amen! :)

Have you prioritized your life well? Do you feel you do too much, over-extending and spreading yourself thin?

May 5

Father God, thank You for Your providence. Like a father, You grant to us what we need to do Your will in our lives- whether it be just enough for ourselves, a family, our neighbors or the greater global community. Whatever we have is not really ours but has been entrusted to us for a little while, with the expectation that we share and multiply whatever has been given to us. The fact of the matter is that if we are not faithful with little, we will not be faithful with much. And in Your Kingdom's economy, whatever little that has been entrusted to us during our stay here on earth will be taken away and given to the one who was faithful with his talents. Lord, open our eyes to see all the opportunities to serve our neighbors and put to good use the talents and resources You have blessed us with- for we are blessed to be a blessing to others. In Jesus' mighty name, we pray. Amen! :)

How have you been a blessing towards others with the blessings God has entrusted to you?

May 6

Dear God, thank You for wanting to be with us. While all the world's religions talk about man's search for You, Christianity is Your search for man. Jesus was the manifestation of Your desire to be with Your people- exemplifying complete, perfect and intense love. A God full of glory and lacking nothing, choosing to give that all up to come down to the level of His own creation, subject to all the hurts and pains that is part of normal life. A life that is not immune to thirst, hunger and fatigue to name a few. Jesus exemplified a love that kept loving even in the face of rejection, betrayal and ridicule of the very same people He came down to save. It is Your desire to be with us- Emmanuel- that we faithfully meet You at the tabernacle at every breaking of bread. May we meet You half way, with a contrite heart so that our spirits can become a live again- for one day with you in Your house is better than a thousand years elsewhere. In Jesus' sweet name, we pray. Amen! :)

How have you met Jesus half-way? Do you attend mass regularly?

May 7

Father God, thank You for the practice of discipline. Just like we know that those who are faithful with little will be faithful with a lot, we know that it's the little things that count. It is the practice with something small and trivial that produces great and amazing champions. It is not the meat that we give up for Lent that will make us saints. It is not the chocolate that we give up that will enable us to conquer mountains. It's the art of giving up something small that we are tempted to do in order to strengthen our will so that we can stand strong in the face of bigger temptation. It's acting in faith that our small little sacrifice today when surrendered into Your Hands will nurture the little Saint that's growing inside. It's believing that the little that we have can be multiplied when given to You. Lord, may we give up something this Lent that will ultimately lead us closer to You and strengthen our walk towards holiness. In Jesus' name we pray, amen!

:)

What small thing have you given up in order to stand strong in greater temptation?

May 8

Father God, thank You for having everything under control. Even if we mess up, You are greater than our inadequacies. We can trust that You will supernaturally send Your angels or orchestrate a situation that will fall in accordance to Your will for our lives. Though we may get tempted to take matters into our own hands, may we humble ourselves and let You take the reins. Often times we feel that the weight of the world is on our shoulders- Lord, in these trying times, quiet our hearts to tune directly to You. Still our minds to channel only thoughts that are pleasing to You. Lord, when our lives look like a mess, may we have the faith that You can make something beautiful out of the chaos. In Jesus precious name, we pray. Amen!

Have you ever felt that God cannot make something beautiful out of the mess you made? How has God proven you wrong and made something even more beautiful than you could ever imagine?

May 9

Father God, thank You for casting out all fear.
More than anything You wrote in Your Word,
You instruct us to "fear not". You didn't negate
the fact that there will be situations in life
that may trigger a sense of fear but You
command us to not fear regardless of the
situation. First and foremost, Your Word reminds
us that no one can be against us and succeed
when You are on our side. Secondly, Your Word
tells us that no weapon that is formed against
us will prosper. Finally, Your Word explains that
we should not fear man for You are our helper.
May all these promises provide comfort in the
midst of intense fear. While perfect love casts
out all fear, may we rest in the knowledge that
we are loved by You and that there is nothing
to fear in this life- but in everything we
surrender to You. In Jesus' powerful name we
pray. Amen! :)

What kind of fear have you experienced
lately? Were you able to surrender it to
God?

May 10

Father God, thank You for caring. Although You are an infinite God, You care about us finite humans. Though You created the immense universe with all its wonders, You are mindful of us petty people and our problems. Though You carry the weight of the world on Your shoulders, You tell us to cast all our burdens on You. Though we think that You have no time to hear about our problems, You wait for us patiently in the blessed sacrament and in prayer. Though we tend to exaggerate any minor issue, You understand our inadequacies and with open and loving arms. Lord, thank You for easing our fears and anxieties, assuring us that everything is under Your control. In Jesus' mighty name, we pray. Amen! :)

How has God cared for you lately? Have you given Him all your fears and worries?

May 11

Father God, thank You for having such high standards. Though we can never attain holiness by our own efforts, we can still strive to be perfect as You, our Father is perfect. You are not satisfied with mere "behavior modification" but rather a transformation of the heart. It's not enough to not commit murder but You command us to not even harbor anger in our hearts towards a brother, for that is committing murder in our hearts. It is not enough to not commit adultery, but rather we must instill clean and pure thoughts about others in our minds, respecting them to be our brothers and sisters in Christ, and not reducing them to mere objects to be used. It's not enough to refrain from evil activity but You command us to do acts of charity, taking care of our neighbors and meeting their needs. Lord, mold our hearts to be warm hearts of love and not hatred or fear. Grant us the strength, persistence and patience to strive for the level of holiness You desire to bless us with- for achieving holiness is the only time we are ever "whole". In Jesus' awesome name we pray. Amen! :)

What high standard have you been struggling with or striving for lately?

May 12

Father God, thank You for the supernatural gift of forgiveness. What separates us from the rest of the world is the ability to forgive and forget. While the rest of the world promotes sweet revenge, You teach us to love our enemies. While we are inclined to become bitter, You tell us to keep our focus on You so that You can sweeten our heart. While the world teaches us to carry the weight of the world and hold grudges, You instruct us to surrender everything to You so that you can liberate our souls. Lord, help our feeble hearts be directed towards You at all times even when the going gets tough- remaining gentle and kind to those that cause us harm. In Jesus' mighty name, we pray. Amen! :)

Who have you forgiven and released from bitterness lately?

May 13

Dear Jesus, thank You for giving us Your
Mother. Being Our Lady of Tears and Sorrows,
we can be comforted to know that our Mother
cries with us when we cry. She is right there
wiping away our tears just like any mother
would. Though we may face many hardships in
our lives, we can know for certainty that Mary
was not exempt from suffering as her calling
was difficult and her soul was pierced. When
she said "yes" at the Annunciation, she didn't
know exactly what she was getting herself into
but she knew she was serving the Lord and that
is all that matters. Though the road was bumpy
and she suffered much, she is now in Heaven
providing comfort and direction to her children-
and we can cry out to Mary when we need that
motherly attention. May we be more like our
mother, humble and gentle in spirit with a heart
willing to serve the Lord, no matter the cost. In
Jesus' gentle name we pray. Amen! :)

What is your relationship with Mary like? Do
you receive the motherly attention that she is
willing to give? How can we be more like Mary in
our approach to life?

May 14

Father God, thank You for being sufficient.
When trials come our way, we are tempted to
run to people for help before ever seeking Your
face first. Your word tells us that one who
trusts in man is cursed and one that trusts in
You is blessed. Often times we feel that
everything depends on our abilities which leads
to anxiety, rather than surrendering to Your will
in our lives and living in complete freedom.
Often times we limit You and all that You can
do and try to take matters into our own hands.
Often times we doubt Your love for us and
decide to find love elsewhere, leaving us
depraved. Lord, in these toughest of times, make
Your love shine brighter to capture our
attention and not seek consolation in man or in
material. May we run to You when we are
desperate, with complete confidence that You
will deliver for our good. In Jesus' mighty name,
we pray. Amen!! :)

How has God been sufficient in your life today?

But he said to me, "My grace is sufficient for you, for my
power is made perfect in weakness." Therefore I will boast all
the more gladly about my weaknesses, so that Christ's power
may rest on me" – 2 Corinthians 12:9

Father God, thank You for Your forgiving mercy and grace. While being in full relationship with You, we have everything, yet we tend to rebel and flirt with sin. Instead of being happy in the shepherd's fold, we want to know what's out there and experience it for ourselves. Instead of following You in complete joy and safety, we want to do things our way because we think we know best. Instead of following Your lead in the dance of life, we step on Your toes and insist on leading. Lord, humble us as Your children to listen and obey for that is the road to true peace and happiness. And if we have strayed far off from Your fold, Lord, break through to our hearts to stop, turn around and come back to You. In Jesus' loving name, we pray. Amen! :)

How have you tried to do things your way? How did it compare to trusting God and sticking to His plan?

May 16

Father God, thank You for Your subtle blessings. Often times we miss the miracles You send our way because it is not packaged in the way we expect it to be. More often than not, we cry and pout that You don't answer our prayers if we don't get what we want. Many times we tell You how You should bless us rather than humbly accept the blessings You impart to us. We are so busy and preoccupied that we miss the little gentle touch and the quiet whisper of Your Spirit, gently guiding us down the path of righteousness. Lord, open our eyes to see the many miracles that surround us on a daily basis and to be gracious for the blessings that You pour down on us, especially the ones that we don't expect. In Jesus' name we pray. Amen! :)

What subtle blessings have you missed lately? How can you be more mindful of all the blessings imparted on you each day?

May 17

Father God, thank You for purifying our minds daily to be holy and pleasing in Your sight. In a world that constantly competes for our attention, we must exercise discipline to focus on what is good. Although there may be 100 things that may make us sad or downtrodden, there are a 1000 things that we can and should be happy about. Instead of focusing on what's wrong, we must learn to focus on what's right. Instead of seeing the cup half empty, we should see the cup half full. At the end of the day, it's all about perspective. Life is 10% of what happens to us and 90% of our attitude and responses to what happens to us. Today, Lord, grant us the strength to take captive our thoughts so that we can make them holy and pleasing in Your sight. In Jesus' precious name we pray. Amen! :)

How has your mind been purified lately? Have your thoughts been holy and pleasing to the Lord?

Father God, thank You for the journey of life. Life is not about the destination but the journey to the destination. Often times we rush through things just to get it done. We rush through our childhood to become adults, but then when we're adults we wish we were children again. We rush through school to work, but then when we work, we wish we were students again. We rush through life to get to heaven, but when we look back, we realized that we rushed through everything and have not stopped to appreciate each moment. While it's good to keep your eye on the prize, we must remember that sanctification is a journey and not a destination. No matter what we may be going through, we must continually remind ourselves of Your love and that every situation, whether good or bad, is an opportunity to exercise the virtues we have been blessed with. Lord, may we grab the opportunity of today to self-reflect and find ways to bring You glory. In Jesus' name, we pray. Amen! :)

Have you been rushing through life or been appreciating each and every moment?

May 19

Father God, thank You for the gift of faith. While we are tempted to not believe it until we see it, You teach us to have faith, believing even though we don't see it. While everything looks grim and bleak around us, faith is believing that someway, somehow there is light at the end of the tunnel. While the world teaches us to operate in the natural, You teach us to have faith and operate in the supernatural. Faith fills in the gap of uncertainty and liberates us to live freely without the weight of worry. When we are tempted to work continuously to resolve all the problems of our lives, You remind us that resting is actually an act of faith, trusting that You will meet us half way. Lord, remind us today that Your grace is still shining above the clouds and we only have to wait in faith that everything will work together for our good. In Jesus' mighty name, we pray. Amen! :)

How has faith played out in your life?

Father God, thank You for the gift of unity.
Just like the perfect unity demonstrated by the
relationship You have with Your Son, may we live
out that unity in all areas of our lives. As Your
children, may we walk closely with Your Son so
that we can look more and more like Him, yet
still embody our distinct personalities. In
marriage, may the two become one flesh, united
in both mind and spirit, acting as one entity, but
yet, 2 persons. As Your Church, may we be
united in terms of theology and practice, acting
as one entity composed of many parts, making a
difference in the world as the hands and feet of
your Son. Lord, may we realize that our
personalities blossom most when our minds and
spirits are united to You. Help us to seek and do
what is most pleasing in Your sight. In Jesus'
name we pray. Amen! :)

How have you been *distinctly* unified, still
harboring your unique personality but in
conjunction with others for a greater purpose?

May 21

Father God, thank You for the gift of values. When the world is in a state of confusion, not knowing when to draw the line, You bless us with set rules and guidelines to give us direction. When the world lives in a state of gray, not knowing what is right and what is wrong, You give us standards to live by. When the world accepts any action to justify the means to the end, You clearly tell us that no wrong can ever fix a wrong. Freedom is not the ability to do whatever we want but the ability to live freely- and boundaries of values help us not to fall off to the wayside. Lord, help us to embrace these boundaries not as a means of restriction but as a means of liberation- and may we exercise these values to the best of our ability. In Jesus' precious name, we pray. Amen!

:)

What values have been liberating to you lately? How has it provided clarity in the world's current state of confusion?

May 22

Father God, thank You for making Yourself known to us. Being born on this rock which is floating in space brings one to wonder the purpose of their existence. Assertions of theism appeal to us, but positions of atheism flirt with our minds, with the clear intention of stealing our devotion to You. Though all of creation scream the intelligence behind Your design, we are still tempted to believe that nothing created us. Though You explicitly tell us that we were created for a purpose, we still struggle with the ideology that we have significance. Though there are many acts of charity, love and kindness in this world, the immense amount of suffering blinds us from the grace that surrounds us. May we see You today in the gentle breeze through the trees, Your promises and through the love in this world that counteracts the evil. Lord, help us to see and embrace our identity as a beautiful child of God, created with a purpose of loving You and loving others. In Your precious name we pray. Amen! :)

How has God made Himself known to you lately? Do you struggle with mainstream thought and ideologies?

Father God, thank You for the gift of hope.
Hope is that little light at the end of the
tunnel. When everything around us seems to
turn in on us, enveloping us in darkness, we fix
our gaze on the tiny light up ahead. That means
we don't stop to look around, dwell on all that is
going wrong in our lives, but to ignore all the
negativity and choose to focus on the positive.
It means to keep our eyes on the prize and not
get distracted by anything that tries to drag us
down. It means to believe with faith that we
will get to that light which will be worth the
fight. Lord, may we fix our eyes on You as You
are that tiny light that gets us through our
days, with full expectancy that we will be
reunited with You at the end of days. Until
then, grant us the strength to keep pushing
forward with Your hope instilled deep into our
hearts. In Your name we pray. Amen! :)

What kinds of little lights of hope have been
giving you strength to push through?

Father God, thank You for the gift of redemption. Redemption is the act of restoring to goodness that which has been lost or has been faulted. While this society has taught us to throw something away if it's broken, You teach us to fix it instead. With divorce rates ranking sky high, instead of dissolving this sacramental bond, You are in the business of restoring broken relationships for Your greater glory. With culture being infiltrated with pagan rituals, instead of burning everything down, You turn holidays such as Easter and Christmas into celebrations of You in lieu of pagan gods. With us continuously making mistakes and falling short, instead of neglecting us sinners and cutting us off, You decide to make us saints. With all of humanity turning our back on You towards sin, instead of destroying all of mankind, You decide to save what was lost and die for our freedom. Thank You for being in the business of redemption- Lord, direct our hearts toward You so that we can allow You to do what You do best- redeeming us so that we are free from sin. In Jesus' name, we pray. Amen! :)

What has God been redeeming in your life lately?

Father God, thank You for Truth. Contrary to popular belief, there is only one truth in the world and that truth is exclusive. Something cannot be right and wrong at the same time. It's either right or it's wrong. Just like pregnancy, you're either pregnant or you're not- you cannot be partially pregnant. Moral relativism has caused much confusion in our generation and as a result, the grip on our moral compass has been lost. Even if 99% of society says 2+2 is 5, that doesn't mean 2+2 equals 5; it just means that 99% of society is wrong. And it is in times like these that we have to firmly stand our ground, defending what we know to be truth. Lord, grant us strength and clarity to confidently stand for what we believe to be true, even if we're standing alone. In Jesus' mighty name, we pray. Amen! :)

What is your understanding of Truth? Do you acknowledge that there is only 1 Truth or do you feel that truth is relative? How can we boldly stand for what we believe to be true?

May 26

Father God, thank You for stilling our hearts. While life will always be a challenge, we can either be drowning in the waters of life, or learn how to float comfortably, trusting that You have everything under control. When life takes its twists and turns, may we enjoy the ride rather than dread what's around the corner. Life can either be a thriller, throwing at us fast balls and curve balls, keeping our lives exciting- or it can be a nightmare, something we dread to see or experience, draining from us the essence of life. Lord, help us to enjoy this roller coaster ride called life, with our arms spread out wide, soaking in all the thrill, trusting that You have everything under control. In Jesus' name we pray. Amen! :)

Has your life been more like a thriller or a nightmare? How can you enjoy this rollercoaster of life more?

May 27

Father God, thank you for the sacrifices of all the soldiers in wars past that have fought for our freedom so that we can love You freely and openly. Just as Your Son died for our freedom 2000 years ago, He conquered death on our behalf. May we remember those that have fought for us so that we can live. On this Pentecost weekend and Memorial Day weekend, we have a lot to ponder over and be grateful for. May we never take one single breath for granted. In Jesus' name, Amen.

As freedom isn't free, what can you do to show gratitude towards Veterans and those that have fallen today?

Father God, thank You for the gift of prudence.
Though we ask that You would not lead us into
temptation, often times we can play a role in
preventing temptation from coming our way. If
we struggle with sexual sin, we can take steps
towards removing ourselves from environments
that are conducive to falling in sin. If we
struggle with alcoholism or drug addiction, we
can take preemptive actions that minimizes our
interaction with alcohol and drugs so that we
won't even be tempted. If we struggle with
anger, we can learn to identify what makes us
angry so that we can address it before it even
gets out of control. We have learned from Your
Son that it is better to pluck out our eye or
chop our hand if they cause us to sin, for it is
better to be maimed than to be thrown into the
fire of hell. Lord, help us to self-reflect to
practice prudence and identify areas in our lives
that need modification and grant us the
strength to implement those preventive
measures to avoid sin. In Jesus' powerful name,
we pray. Amen! :)

How have you practiced prudence in
avoiding sins that you regularly get
tempted to commit?

Father God, thank You for the gift of time and space. We may never understand why, but You decide to operate in the physical realm, bounded by time and space. We are entities composed of spirit and body, not just a spirit OR a body but both. You chose to come down from heaven and become human, subject to all the laws of physics that we are subject to. You chose to physically and spiritually die for our physical and spiritual needs, conquering death and granting us the forgiveness of our sins. Undoubtedly, things happen slower bounded by time and space, where it took 4,000 years for Your Son to enter humanity and redeem us, it took 33 years for Him to grow up and complete His mission and it'll take however long You decide until the end of time, for the resurrection of the dead to occur. Lord, help us to understand that You are a God of patience and order, so that we can embrace the limitations of time and space, knowing full well that it's part of Your perfect plan for our lives. In Jesus' perfect name we pray. Amen! :)

What is your relationship with space and time like? Are you patient with the limitations it holds?

Dear God, thank You for giving us meaning and purpose. In a world of meaninglessness, it's easy to get caught up with the mundane world, faithfully completing tasks just to complete them. In simply the physical realm with no spiritual component, suffering is meaningless and encouraged to be avoided. In an existential manner, what I do today does not affect anyone else and has no eternal impact. But that certainly is not the case in reality, whether we like to believe it or not. Everything that we do, no matter how trivial it may seem, plays a role in the grand scheme of things. Our sufferings in this life can be offered up to be used for good. Our faithfulness to complete mundane, worldly tasks is not unnoticed in Your eyes and will be rewarded 10-fold. Lord, fill us with the joy of Your salvation as we go about our days, completing the tasks You have entrusted to us, with You in mind. In Jesus' name we pray. Amen!
:)

Do you believe that everything you do has purpose and meaning?

Father God, thank You for the ability to praise Your name. Although it is natural for us to praise You when everything is going well, we must remember that our praise should not be conditional. We were created to praise You with our lives, during the good and the bad; and when we don't is when we lose focus on what's really important. It's easy to praise You when the sun is out and shining but the real challenge is when the storms roll our way. It's easy to glorify You when things go according to plan, but the real glory comes when life gets tough, yet we continue to stick by Your side. It's easy to be happy when everything is peachy but You are most pleased when we thank You and bless Your name despite the current situations. Lord, help us to embrace our purpose in glorifying Your name with our lives so that we can live to our utmost potential. In Jesus' sweet name we pray. Amen! :)

Have you been able to praise His name through the good and the bad?

June 1

Father God, thank You for the gift of a human life. Although often times the beauty of a life can be drowned out by all the silly distractions that surround it, a life is still a life. Sure a child may be born out of wed-lock, but that child is just as precious as the one born to wedded parents. Sure a person may have no riches and is as poor as poor can be, but that person is just as valuable in Your eyes as someone who is rolling in wealth. Sure a fetus has not fully developed into a full sized baby, yet that fetus still has a soul and is as loved as the fetus that was given the opportunity to develop into a full sized baby and was given the opportunity at life. No matter the circumstances that surround the instance of life, the dignity of a single human being is worth more than the entire created world. Lord, grant us the eyes to see the beauty of every person's life- as someone unrepeatable and precious in Your eyes- and help us to give every person the opportunity to reach their fullest potential in life. In Jesus' mighty name we pray. Amen! :)

How do you view every created being placed on this earth, born and unborn? Do you see them the same way God sees them?

Father God, thank You for giving us options. It doesn't take too much time on this earth to figure out that life is the accumulation of decisions that we make on a daily basis. Decisions that bring us closer to Christ or draw us further from Christ. Decisions that increase our trust and reliance on You and decisions that make us a slave to uncertainty and anxiety. Decisions that increase our happiness and decisions that rob us of our joy and drags us down into darkness. Although things may happen to us that we have no control over and we would have changed it if it were up to us, we can still make the decision to be happy, to be free and to trust that You have our best interest in mind. Lord, grant us the strength to make the right decisions that bring us closer to You. In Jesus' mighty name we pray. Amen! :)

What decisions have you made recently that has brought you closer or further away from Christ?

June 3

Father God, thank You for being God. As simple as it sounds, You are God and we are not. Until we fully grasp that concept, we will continuously try to play Your role in our lives. We try to control things we have no control over. We try to tell You what You should and should not do. We try to change Your Commandments and Your Law to fit what we think and feel best. But what ends up happening is that we become overwhelmed, tired, discouraged, distraught, confused and ultimately unhappy. Lord, teach us to humbly accept Your ways for we know it's the path towards happiness. Help us to surrender to Your will, accepting anything that may come along the way- and may we come to realize that You are God and nothing is too big for You to handle. In Jesus' name we pray. Amen! :)

How can you see God as God and you as the created more clearly? How can you let God be God more in your life?

June 4

Father God, thank You for Your peace and rest. When there are a million things to do and many more deadlines to abide to, we can decide to stop and step out of all the chaos and just appreciate the moment. It is only then that we grasp the essence of our humanity- that we are not just mere pawns in the rat race of life- but rather an important being that You are intensely mindful of. It's easy to think that everything depends on us- but, in reality, it's never depended on us because it is You who keeps us going, You who grants us the breath of life to wake up in the mornings, You who provides us with just what we need at the right time. Lord, help us to slow down today and simply appreciate the moment that You have blessed us with, while trusting that everything will fall into place. In Jesus' sweet name, we pray. Amen! :)

How can you step out of the rat race of life and simply appreciate the moment?

June 5

Dear Jesus, thank You for being the Good Shepherd. As mere little lambs in this rough and difficult life, it's comforting to know that You are the Shepherd whom we have grown to know and trust. It is Your voice that draws us in when we go astray. It is Your staff that protects us when harm comes our way. It is You who would lay down Your life to save ours. You are the God that is mindful of even the little lamb that's falling behind in the back. And if that little lamb should get lost, we can rest assured that You would leave the 99 to find the one. God, help us to remember that You have not forgotten about us in this rough life of ours but are faithfully leading us down the path to life everlasting. In Jesus' name we pray. Amen!

:)

How has God been the Good Shepherd in your life? Have you strayed away from the fold only to find yourself back?

June 6

Father God, thank You for mentors. In a life with so many possibilities and different directions to go, we all need mentors in our lives. Although we may think and feel we know what's best, there will always be someone who knows the ropes better. It takes humility to stop, listen and do what our elders are advising us to do. It takes wisdom to identify the mentors in our lives and cling to them. It takes courage to trust the mentors in our lives, believing that they will do their best to steer us in the right direction. And although mentors tend to be older because they have experienced more and have gone so far with fruit to show for it, there is no age criteria to being a mentor, for we can learn just as much from our children as we can learn from our elders. Children know how to trust without limits, teens and young adults know how to live and embrace the moment, and older adults know how to let go- nevertheless, we can all mentor each other in one way or another. Lord, help us to see the mentors in our lives so that we can learn from them and help us walk closer to You. In Your precious name we pray. Amen! :)

Who are the mentors in your life? What can you learn from children, teens, adults and elders?

June 7

Father God, thank You for being above Time. As mere humans, we are subject to many limitations such as time and space- but You, being an infinite being, are outside of all these restraints and essentially can do all that You please. In an era of deadlines and time constraints, we are constantly racing against the clock, hoping to extract more time out of a minute. As a means to get more time to do what we think is necessary, we may feel the need to miss Mass because that is precious time that can be used for something else. We may feel a need to cut corners in relationships and push loved ones aside in order to complete what we set out to do. We may even feel the need to cut back on ourselves, such as our health, where we don't eat, sleep or exercise properly in order to get ahead. Though all these temptations may rise, may we always remember that when we tag team with You, we can go further than when we try to do everything by our own efforts. Lord, grant us the peace and serenity to invest in what is important to us despite all the pressing urgencies that try to rob us of our precious time. In Jesus' name, we pray. Amen! :)

How have you cut back on what is truly important in your life in order to do more of what is "urgent"?

June 8

Father God, thank You for the gifts of Your Holy Spirit. In this world where the ruler is Satan, we are constantly at war for peace. While You desire to bless us with gifts of love, peace and joy, Satan seeks to steal, kill and destroy us. While You calm the storm in our hearts, Satan seeks to stir up the storms. While You promise to bring us to green pastures and still waters, Satan seeks to devour us like a prowling lion. Lord, may we understand that we will always be fighting this spiritual battle but we can decide to put on Your Armor when we start the day and fight with You on our side. May You strengthen us as we fight this battle of life. In Jesus' name we pray. Amen! :)

June 9

Father God, thank You for the opportunities to serve. Until we finally realize that we were created to serve one another, we will never achieve complete joy and happiness. In a society which constantly thinks about oneself, it is difficult to refrain from that mentality and lovingly and willingly give of ourselves. In a society whose main goal is happiness, it is ironic that it has not come to the conclusion that serving others wholeheartedly leads to fulfillment. In a society that is competitive in nature, it has achieved and obtained so much, yet is so deprived of true richness and satisfaction. Lord, open up our eyes to opportunities today to serve others, for when we serve the least of these, we are in fact serving You.

June 10

Father God, thank You for marriage. Marriage is the holy matrimony of a man and a woman perfectly designed to reflect Your love for us. The love between a man and a woman naturally will bring forth new life- and it is through the relationships developed between the spouses and the child that imperfectly resemble the relationship of the Holy Trinity. Marriage is meant to give us a glimpse of the perfect love that You have for us. Marriage is the continual love between 2 imperfect beings despite the continual disappointments or failures. Marriage is the constant act of forgiveness for the sake of maintaining pure and true love. Marriage is an earthly creation, specifically designed to reveal the perfect love that awaits for us in heaven. Lord, may we embrace the institution of marriage as a holy sacrament, designed to temporarily bring a little bit of heaven down on earth. In Your precious name we pray. Amen! :)

" Submit to one another out of reverence for Christ."
- Ephesians 5:21

June 11

Father God, thank You for that glimmer of hope. Although we may be surrounded by darkness, we must find that glimmer of light and cling to it. That glimmer may be that light at the end of the tunnel, informing us that the end is approaching. That glimmer may be the understanding that the sun will shine after the storm passes. That glimmer may be knowing that it is darkest right before the dawn and that the day will break soon enough. Although life will not fail to surprise us with twists and turns, it's up to us to find peace within the chaos- and that glimmer of hope makes that possible. Lord, reveal to us the little things that make us smile, which promise us a brighter future. In Your name we pray. Amen! :)

June 12

Thank you for opportunities to grow. When we ask for patience, You give us situations to exercise our patience. When we ask for endurance, You give us trying times that require us to persevere and cling to Your side. When we ask for peace, You give us situations that force us to focus on the positives and fix our eyes on You. Lord, may we never miss the opportunities to grow so that the virtues that are already in us can be strengthened, making us look more and more like You. In Jesus' mighty name, we pray. Amen! :)

June 13

Father God, thank You for the ability to believe.
Just as Your servant, St. Augustine explained,
we don't try to understand in order to believe
but that we believe in order that we
understand. In a world that cannot be explained
by the mere physical, we must be aware and
account for the supernatural. However, this can
be difficult as the supernatural cannot be easily
measured or observed as the natural world. By
its very nature, it escapes our natural forms of
measure and observations and even escapes our
finite understanding according to the world
around us. But at the same time, the entirety of
our existence cannot be explained by just the
physical. The phenomena of life- encompassed
by the physical and spiritual realms- which
occur on a daily basis cannot be contained by
our mere human minds; and this is why we must
belief in order to completely understand. Lord,
may we exercise the natural capacity of our
beings to believe, and believe with our whole
hearts. In Your name, we pray. Amen! :)

How has your ability to believe impacted
your understanding of the word around
us?

Father God, thank You for making life significant. It doesn't take much for us to realize and become aware of the brevity, frailty and triviality of life. Just as Your Word informs us, our lives are but vapor in the wind, here today and gone tomorrow. In a very existential perspective, our lives hold no meaning but a mere struggling under the hot sun, working all our lives only to die one day. With no consideration of the spiritual component in our lives, this worldview is very discouraging; but You, our God, give us substantial meaning to our lives. No suffering is unnoticed and no good deed is unrewarded. Everything is accounted for, giving us every motivation to do our very best in this life that we lead, for Your glory. Lord, may we be aware of the brevity of life, where all of our days are numbered, strengthening us to act as if every day counted.

How has knowing that our lives are significant impacted the way you live? Do you live with more purpose and meaning?

June 15

Father God, thank You for pruning our lives in order to produce more fruit. Pruning entails cutting away dead areas of our lives to give room for more growth. It even entails cutting away "partially" dead areas that may seem to contribute to our happiness but is really preventing us from reaching our full potential. Parts of our lives that we need to do away with to prevent us from sinning, for its better to be maimed than to sin and be thrown into the unquenchable fire. Pruning is removing the clutter from our lives that impedes in our productivity. Lord, give us the wisdom to know what to prune away in our lives and the strength to do so, in order to serve You more fully. In Your name we pray. Amen!

How has God been pruning areas of your life to produce more fruit?

"He cuts off every branch in me that bears no fruit, while every branch that does bear fruit he prunes so that it will be even more fruitful."
-John 15:2

June 16

Father God, thank You for opportunities of generosity. Although it is easy for a wealthy person to fall into sin, having more than we need grants us opportunities to exercise our love and give. A man is only rich if he can share out of surplus- and a man is "poor" if he cannot share, despite having more than enough and yet desires for a little bit more. We are blessed to be a blessing towards others, and when we withhold those blessings, we become poor in spirit because we find it difficult to share. In the same token, it takes real humility to accept people's generosity when it is being offered- for a prideful man would pretend that nothing is wrong only to appear fine but is really hurting inside. Lord, grant us a giving and receiving spirit so that we can be one united family of humanity. In Your name we pray. Amen! :)

What opportunities have you been given to give? And what opportunities have you been given to receive?

June 17

Father God, thank You for the ability to prioritize. In a world of limited resources, we cannot do everything. Very soon we find that our time on earth is limited and what we have is not really ours but lent to us. It is for this reason that we have to determine what deserves of our attention, our efforts, and our resources. And by the same token, we need be aware of that which does NOT deserve our time, attention and effort- namely avenues of sin. We must identify what activities on this earth will have eternal effects and set forth to do them.

We must capitalize on our God-given time, talent and treasure to bring Him glory with our lives, no matter who or what we are. For we know that he who has given everything up for Your kingdom will reap his reward. Therefore, may we live our lives wisely, prioritizing our valuable resources in such a way that will bring You the most glory. In Your precious name we pray. Amen! :)

What in your life deserves more of your time and attention? And what areas in your life do not? How can you shift the priorities in your life to reflect this?

June 18

Father God, thank You for Your guardian angels that protect us on a daily basis. It's silly for us to think that all that we see is all that there is. There is a huge spiritual world that escapes our senses but not our awareness. And this spiritual world is not stagnant or boring but rather exciting and thrilling - with war being fought on a daily basis. A war in which we are unfortunately caught up in the middle. A war that was waged before time between 2 strong but unequal forces, in which the stronger force, namely You, prevails. And as with any war, we must choose sides- for if we don't, a side is automatically chosen for us. Lord, we know that if we're not for You, we are against You. And if we're not gathering for Your kingdom, we are scattering against Your kingdom. May we not let another day pass where we are not actively fighting in this war so that we can, like brave soldiers, fight for a good cause. In Your mighty name we pray. Amen! :)

How aware are you of the spiritual world and the battles that take place on a daily basis? How can you be more in tune?

June 19

Father God, thank You for the gift of forgiveness. Forgiveness is not an option but a necessity of life. There is not one person who has not been transgressed against nor one person that has not transgressed against another- hence the need for forgiveness. Forgiveness is the door to liberation, releasing ourselves from the chains of resentment- whereas maintaining a grudge is draining and enslaving of no one else but the one holding the grudge. Furthermore, forgiveness of others opens the door to answered prayers and forgiveness on our part from You. No one is without sin for all have fallen short of Your glory - yet You offer us forgiveness and a cleansing of our souls as long as we offer the same mercy towards others that have wronged us. Lord, soften our hearts towards forgiveness of anyone who is needing forgiveness, for our sake and for the sake of our brother and sisters. In Your sweet name we pray. Amen! :)

How has forgiveness been a gift in your life? What chains broke when you forgave your neighbor or yourself?

June 20

Father God, thank You for being that solid rock upon which we stand. Just like any structure, it is built on a strong foundation to support the rest of the structure in the midst of peace and chaos. In gentle breezes, it is undisturbed; in moderate storms, the structure is challenged and may bend back and forth, but if the foundation is strong, the structure will stand; in severe storms, which are expected to come, the structure may experience some damage, but a strong foundation facilitates the reconstruction process. This simple description illustrates the overall process of life, a process of strengthening, breaking down and building back up again- but the foundation sets the stage for it all. Lord, may we build our lives on You and Your truths, trusting You no matter what our circumstances may look like. In Jesus' powerful name, we pray. Amen! :)

What is your foundation like? Is it strong built on the truth of God or is it weak built on the lies of the enemy?

June 21

Father God, thank You for the gift of heaven.
Although the concept of heaven escapes our
human understanding, we are assured of its
existence through Your Word. In a purely
materialistic society, where everything
eventually fades away and is degraded, it's
difficult to imagine that there is a spiritual
dwelling place for our souls for all of eternity.
The idea of heaven may be disturbing to an
existentialist, but the promise of heaven gives
hope to the suffering. Heaven is a place where
suffering will be no more, where our souls will
be completely satisfied in communion with our
Lord, where we will all unite in communion with
the Saints worshipping with one voice, singing
Your praise. Essentially, heaven will be Utopia,
where everything is what it was always meant
to be. Lord, may we be strengthened by the
promise of heaven during our journey on earth.
In Jesus' name we pray. Amen! :)

What is your relationship with heaven like? Do
you await for it in anticipation or is it just an
afterthought?

June 22

Father God, thank You for Your truth. In a
world which is ruled by the Father of Lies, it is
easy to be caught up with distorted self-images
and world views. Every step towards truth, we
are bombarded with a set of lies intended to
bring us back into darkness. Just like the field
of research is a slow, tedious and arduous task
towards seeking a better understanding of the
world around us, we must be diligent scientists
regarding Your truth for our lives. Your truth
sets us free, enables us to be the best that we
can be, and brings us closer to Your Son, who is
essentially the Way, the Truth and the Life.
Lord, help us to stay focused on Your truth and
not be distracted by all the lies that surround
us on a daily basis. In Your name we pray.
Amen! :)

What lies have you been believing lately
about yourself and/or the world around
you? What promises and truth can be
used to combat those lies?

June 23

Father God, thank You for holy obedience rather than legalism. Holy obedience is following Your laws and statutes with love and reverence rather than grudgingly obeying to avoid punishment. Obeying with love allows us to live life to the fullest, allowing us to reap the benefits of following Your good Law. But obeying simply because we "have to" creates a bitter heart and spirit, of which may eventually turn away from You. Your law was made for us, Your children, as rules to provide us healthy boundaries that prevent us from straying and getting lost, from falling off the side of the precipice, from going too far and hurting ourselves. Your law is the staff that keeps us together and safe. Sheep see the staff of their shepherd not as something to fear and avoid but rather as a point of reference, something that keeps them safe. Lord, may we learn to abide by Your law out of love and reverence so that we can come to know You as our loving Father. In Your name we pray. Amen! :)

Has your relationship with God been more of holy obedience or legalism? Do you attend mass begrudgingly or with joy?

June 24

Father God, thank You for good and bad fruit.
Often times, we will encounter people who do
not have the best intentions in mind and simply
wish to cause destruction. You tell us that we
can discern these wolves in sheep's clothing from
good sheep through the fruits in their lives. Do
they have a loving monogamous marriage with
faithful and obedient children? Are they gentle,
kind and giving? Can they keep a stable job? Are
they known for good character traits or
notorious for sin? What is their relationship with
You, our Father? Do they regularly attend mass
and frequent the sacraments to become better
people or do they find it a waste of time? The
first signs of the state of the heart are the
fruits in one's lives- just as the first thing that
is foregone in a tree when infected are the good
fruits. Lord, open our eyes to see the fruits of
people to help us discern who to trust and who
to help generate good fruit again. In Your name
we pray. Amen! :)

What are some of the good and bad fruits
that you see in the people around you?
How have they been able to help you
discern the wolves from the sheep?

June 25

Father God, thank You for the significance of
actions. Very quickly, we realize that words are
cheap and it takes real courage to act on what
we say we will do. It's one thing to say we
desire to follow You and Your ways- it's another
thing to actually do. Essentially, we must "put
our money where our mouths are". Of course,
we must first learn what it is that You expect
of us, in order that we know what we should do.
For that, we must be persistent in reading and
listening to Your word. But it doesn't end there,
we must activate our spirits to actually move in
the direction of holiness and righteousness. Lord,
help us to not only know what we must do but
also act on what we must do- so that we can
effectively build our lives on solid ground. In
Your name, we pray. Amen! :)

Have you been practicing what you have been
preaching? What areas can use more action and
less talk in your life?

June 26

Father God, thank You for the ripple effect. Often times our lives seem so small and minuscule, that we don't see the impact we have on people's lives. Our existence seems so trivial that we don't see our importance in the world around us. But we know from experience that we may tremendously impact people in such a way that we may never understand. In fact, we may positively contribute to someone's life that can be life changing and we may never even know it. Just like the ripple effect, the small kind gesture that we do today may tremendously impact someone along the line- even someone we have never met. Although the direct effects of our lives may be small, that does not necessarily mean the indirect effects are small. Even the smallest pebble can create such incredible and magnificent ripples. Lord, may we never underestimate the impact we can have on the world around us and teach us to be small pebbles with big aspirations. In Jesus' name we pray. Amen! :)

What ripple effect have you or someone you know had recently?

June 27

Father God, thank You for granting all that we need. Although we constantly complain and beg for more, it takes maturity to stop pouting and start appreciating all that You have already blessed us with. It takes strength to say that I really don't need that because I already have all that I need. It takes a heart full of gratitude to be satisfied with what we already have and not seek for more. And this is not only for material goods but for other needs such as spiritual, physical, mental and emotional fulfillment. Often times we fret when we don't "hear" You, but fail to realize that You speak through Your Word. We complain if we're not as agile as the next, but fail to realize that we are healthy, able and woke up this morning. We worry that we don't know as much as our neighbor, but fail to realize that You have given us amazing brains that can be used for Your glory in any capacity. We pout when we don't get enough love from other people, but fail to realize that our loved ones have never stopped loving us and Your love is all that will need to satisfy our souls. Lord, may we not focus on what we lack but rather on what we have, by Your mercy and grace. In Your precious and sweet name, we pray. Amen! :)

How have you failed to realize that you have all that you need? How can you be more appreciative of what God has blessed you with?

June 28

Father God, thank You for challenges in this life. Sure we may pray for all obstacles to be removed from our lives so that we can live an easy and comfortable life- but we fail to see that it is in obstacles that we have the opportunities to exercise our virtues. When something doesn't go our way, we have the opportunity to be patient and wait upon the Lord. When we encounter a rude neighbor, we have the opportunity to love regardless of the neighbor's actions. When we are in need, it gives the opportunity for another to give generously, out of the abundance that has been given to them. As mere children constantly looking for comfort, we fail to realize the best things in life often times come from challenges encountered along the way. Lord, may we not get frustrated when we encounter obstacles in our lives but rather see them as an opportunity to grow in virtue. In Jesus' name we pray.
Amen! :)

What obstacles have you encountered lately? What blessings can come from those obstacles?

June 29

Father God, thank You for spiritual eyes. In a
world where people tend to see nothing as a
miracle, You give us eyes to see everything as a
miracle. From the development of a human life
in a mother's womb, to the rising and the setting
of the sun over all of creation, to the very fact
that we are alive for yet another day, the truth
of the matter is that we all live a miracle.

Whether we see it is up to us and our
perspective of the world around us. Lord, grant
us the spiritual eyes so that we can see You in
all that we do, see and think. In Your name we
pray. Amen! :)

Have you been able to see miracles all around
you?

Father God, thank You for Your promises. In a world that can easily steal our joy, You replenish our souls with the essence of Your promises. It is Your promises that we cling to when we have nothing else. It is Your promises that restore our hope when everything around us seem bleak. It is Your promises that we stand on when everything else fails. It doesn't take long for us to realize that people are imperfect and will fail us, even our loved ones. So quickly we understand that we live in a battle field, often requiring us to put on our armor before the day even starts. The best thing about Your promises is that it's definitive - where You say "come to me and I WILL give you rest" rather than "I MAY give you rest". Now it's up to us to truly believe it and hold fast to it. Lord, help us to believe You when You promise good to us and may we hold Your promises close to our hearts. In Jesus' name we pray. Amen! :)

What promises have you clung to recently? What promises should you be clinging to?

July 1

Dear God, thank You for giving us the Sabbath. Although You have intended it to be a sacred day of rest, bringing our attention to what really matters in life, man has thwarted its original intention to become a burdensome righteous duty. Jesus said it clearly- You desire mercy not sacrifice, but we often miss the point, which is the essence of "sin". The Sabbath was created for us, not us for the Sabbath- bringing the Sabbath back to its original purpose. Just as You are our Creator, You know exactly what it is that we need, which is why You tell us to keep the Sabbath holy. In order to fully flourish as Your children, we need to keep our focus on You and take the time to rest from our work- that is why You designate a full day as a day of rest. Lord, may we honor the Sabbath as the holy day of rest to the best of our abilities. In Your name we pray. Amen! :)

What is your relationship with the Sabbath as a day of rest like? Do you take the rest that you need every week?

July 2

Father God, thank You for being the root of all good things. In life, we are going to encounter a myriad of emotions and experiences including positive and negative ones. However, we need to be discerning to determine what are from You and what are NOT from You but can be used by You. Often times, living a life of sin can bring us a temporary, short-lived sense of high but a long term effect of misery. Though we may be tempted to say that the good feeling we received was from You, but rather, it was wrapped up sin that seemed like it was from You. Similarly, when "bad" things happen, often times it's due to the sins of others, our sins or just You trying to discipline us like a good Father, pruning us to bear more fruit. But it's up to us to see the lesson You are trying to teach us, accept it and apply it to our lives so that we can walk closer to You in righteousness. Lord, may we be savvy to discern the sin that intends to destroy us from the positive attribute You wish to bless us with. In Jesus' name we pray. Amen! :)

Have you been able to discern the good from the bad wisely? Have you ever mistakened a sin to be something good when it really was not? And vice versa?

July 3

Dear God, thank You for the desire to do Your will. Often times, we try to make sense of what You have us to do, but in our limited understanding, we cannot appreciate the vast wisdom that comes with Your statutes. Even when the Israelites did not understand hygiene and cleanliness, they still obeyed the mandated cleansing rituals, preventing them from contracting and dying from infectious diseases like everyone around them. Just because it doesn't make sense to us in the natural sense to tithe, we still tithe, waiting with expectancy that You will multiply what we have given back to You. Just like we don't understand everything that Your Church mandates, we obey faithfully, believing that it will bring the most life, allowing us to blossom and flourish. Lord, may we willingly obey Your divine mandates, even if they don't make sense to our earthly brains. In Your name we pray. Amen! :)

What mandates and statutes does the Church have and encourage us to live by that you don't understand completely? Do you still follow them?

July 4

Father God, thank You for freedom. Quite ironically, freedom is not necessarily "free" but comes at a great cost. The desire of broken people to control other people is inherent in all of us, and most apparent in those with the power to control. But that is the reason why checks-and-balances were instituted into our constitution, to prevent such tyranny and chaos. Similarly, our spiritual freedom also came with a great cost, with Your body broken and Your blood spilled at the cross. Just as many people take their earthly freedom for granted, we tend to take our spiritual freedom for granted, never really tapping into the spiritual practices to grow closer to You- and we miss out on the spiritual freedom that we can enjoy. Lord, just as we exercise the freedom to live without constraint, may we exercise our freedom to live without spiritual bonds or chains. In Your name we pray. Amen! :)

July 5

Dear God, thank You for joy in unselfishness. Just as St. Mother Teresa once said, we are only as miserable as we are selfish. You engineered us to find joy when we abandon ourselves and focus on others. You wired our spirits to be complete when they are connected to You and not focused on ourselves. You created us to be in community, helping each other as a collective effort and not have individualistic mindsets. We all know that the quickest way to depression is when we live for ourselves because we were never meant to be selfish. It is our fallen nature to be selfish and to seek out for number one. As CS Lewis mentioned, we have all that we need but in our fallen nature, we can't bear the fact that our neighbor may have more than us. Lord, help us to purge this tendency out of us so that we can be less me-centered and more others-centered in order to fulfill our original design and find pure sweet joy. In your name we pray. Amen. :)

How can you be less me-centered and more others-centered in your life?

July 6

Father God, thank You for answering our prayers in the way You find best. Often times, we fret when we don't receive the answers to our prayers in the way we expect, preventing us from seeing the answers in the way You intend to bless us. Just like the man in a major flood looked for Your divine intervention to save him, but failed to see the many boats that were sent to help him. Just like the man looked for Your presence and couldn't "find" You, but failed to see You in the gentle touch of a butterfly. Just like we ask for help with our finances and expect to win the lottery, but fail to see the many opportunities that we are given to work our way out of debt. Lord, may we humble ourselves to see the answers to our prayers in the way You find best for the purpose of our sanctification. In Your name we pray. Amen! :)

What answers to your prayers have been different to what you were expecting? Were you able to see them in time?

July 7

Father God, thank You for the life that results from death. Just like the seed that has to die in order for life to sprout, You call us to die to our selfish desires in order to nurture life that will manifest in our lives.

In a world where we are taught to fight for number one, You teach us to gladly take the lowly position- for the first will be last and the last will be first. In a society where pride is tantamount, You teach us to humble ourselves and admit when we are wrong, or dismiss the petty issue altogether- for it's better to reconcile with your neighbor and re-establish peace than to prolong the argument and create strife. Often times we are prone to sin, but You call us resist temptation and pursue the path of righteousness- for that is what is most important anyways. Lord, help us to die to our sinful nature and keep our focus on You so that life can spring up once again. In Jesus' name we pray. Amen! :)

How have you had to die recently in your life in order for life to come forth?

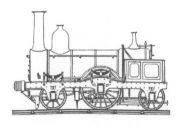

July 8

Father God, thank You for flexibility. Although we wish we can know what's going to happen tomorrow, as mere humans, we cannot. We wish we can control the future but that'll just drive us mad. It is for this reason that we must learn to be flexible and follow wherever Your Spirit may guide us. We may be certain that we want to go down one path, but You know what's best and occasionally You completely shut that door so that we cannot pass through. We can either fret about it and throw a tantrum or we can humbly accept that and walk through the door that You have divinely opened. Lord, give us malleable hearts that can bend easily but not break and be molded into whatever You so desire. Help us to see the open doors that You want us to walk through and may we willingly obey. In Your precious name we pray. Amen! :)

What doors have closed in your life recently? Did another door or window open for you to walk through?

169

July 9

Father God, thank You for being the transcendent source of joy in our lives. In a pleasure-seeking society, we are constantly bombarded with signs and images that promise to make us happier if only we could get the product or service that is being offered. Although those things can provide a temporary sense of high, that quickly dissipates and leaves us right where we started. We are told that happiness comes from people, places and things but we know that sweet joy comes directly from You. Joy is that inherent sense of peace and contentment no matter the circumstances. Joy is the ability to smile when nothing really good has happened recently. Joy is that overwhelming sense of happiness that becomes contagious with anyone we come in contact with. Lord, may we cherish and embrace the inherent joy that transcends any external circumstances that can only come from You. In Your precious name we pray. Amen! :)

Have you felt the difference between happiness and joy? What was it like to be happy and what was it like to be joyful?

July 10

Father God, thank You for the old and the new. Though we may be tempted to just live in the now, we have to look back to see what has made us who we are today. Though we may be focused on current events, we should look back on what's happened before to identify any precedence which may help us today. Though we may be tempted to throw away anything that is old and tarnished, we have to learn to cherish the value of ancient items that increase in worth as time passes. Though we tend to discredit what our elders have to say, we must realize that they are a reservoir of wisdom that needs to be tapped into for the purpose of applying it to our lives and making better decisions. Though we may be tempted to focus on Your New Testament, help us see how the Old Testament holds the mysteries that are revealed in the New Testament, giving a bigger and better picture of Your Kingdom. Lord, help us to see the beauty in both the new and the old, giving us a more holistic view in our lives. In Your name we pray. Amen! :)

What is your relationship like with the old and the new? Do you tend to focus on one more than the other? How can we cultivate a more balanced relaionship with both?

July 11

Father God, thank You for the grace to do as we ought. Though sin and temptation will always be present knocking on our door, and we may stumble and fall occasionally, but the most important thing is to stop, get up, dust off the dirt and to start over. It's when we get stuck in a rut and start walking in the wrong direction that gets us in trouble. As much as You desire to have our hearts' allegiance, You desire even more for us to walk alongside Your Son in obedience and righteousness. Lord, may we see each new day as another opportunity to start afresh, with our minds set on doing right in Your eyes. In Your precious name we pray. Amen! :)

Have you always been able to do as you ought to do? When you didn't, were you able to stop what you were doing, get up and keep going in the right direction?

Father God, thank You for change. As we all know, apart from You, the only constant in life is change. This great paradox of life reveals that no matter what is happening in our lives, things will change, for better and/or for worse. We may be going through a long and terrible storm, but what we fail to realize is that You are in control of that storm and You can change the direction of that storm any minute. The same applies in the other direction- everything may be going really well for us and in a split second, everything can go crashing down. It is in those dramatic times that we draw closer to You, realizing that You are all that we really need. Lord, help us to embrace the inevitable concept of change in our lives, keeping our eyes focused on You, so that when change comes our way, for better or for worse, our foundations will not be shaken. In Your precious name we pray. Amen! :)

What changes have occurred recently? Were they good, bad or neutral changes?

July 13

Father God, thank You for opportunities to share Your love. It won't be long until we encounter another circumstance to love our neighbor. Whether it be as close as family and friends, or as distant as our neighbors across the world in another country, we are presented with a multitude of opportunities to express Your love on a daily basis. Loving someone can look different in every situation as there is no simple formula. Love is simply desiring the best for another. Therefore, if our neighbor lacks, and we have, we love when we share. If our neighbor is sad and overwhelmed, we love when we listen and show we care. If our neighbor is sick and needs physical help, we love when we do our best to nurse them back to health. If our family members don't have a personal relationship with You, we love when we share that love and joy You grant us so that they can have the same relationship with their Creator. It is no mistake that Your Son simplified the Law into 2 important commandments: to love You with all our heart, mind and soul and to love our neighbor as we love ourselves- for Love is the powerful essence that drives us to do good, whatever may be pleasing in Your sight. Lord, please grant us hearts that would compel us to express our love in any way that a situation would present itself. In Your precious name we pray. Amen! :)

How have you loved your neighbor recently?

July 14

Dear God, thank You for delivering us from slavery. Slavery is anything that keeps us from reaching our full potential as Your children. By its very nature, sin enslaves us, whether we know it or not. The sin that makes us jealous and ungrateful, prevents us from seeing all the blessings in our lives. The sin that makes us greedy and reluctant to help each other when someone is in need. The sin that oppresses another and prevents our neighbor from rising up in life. The sin that cultivates strife in the household rather than nurturing peace and love. The sin that harbors bitterness and resentment rather than releasing the pain to You so that You can vindicate and establish justice. Lord, may we release all that enslaves us, refraining from sin, so that we can relish in the good and peaceful life You promised us. In Your precious name we pray. Amen! :)

What sins have been enslaving you recently? How can you break away from those sins?

"But thanks be to God that, though you used to be slaves to sin, you have come to obey from your heart the pattern of teaching that has now claimed your allegiance."- Romans 6:17

July 15

Father God, thank You for mornings. Mornings are reminders that we can always start afresh and we can leave the old in the night. Mornings wake us up with a new day full of possibilities ahead of us, good and bad but we must trust that You will strengthen us to tackle the bad and embrace the good. Mornings provide light to the long and dark night, bringing warmth and healing to whatever ails the body, mind and soul. Mornings bring joy and laughter, even if sorrow lasted throughout the night, reminding us to put out the old and bring in the new, each 24 hours, 7 days a week. Lord, there will be many times that we fall into bad habits throughout our days but each morning You provide us with the opportunity to get back into gear towards holiness. In Your name we pray. Amen! :)

July 16

Father God, thank You for humility. Humility is the virtue that enables us to live in peace with one another- accepting each other's flaws, understanding that we have flaws of our own. Humility is the practice of stopping and admitting when we are wrong, when pride wants us to keep pretending we are right. Humility is the art of apologizing to make amends when pride wants us to burn bridges and go our own way. Humility is the tendency to think of others before ourselves, when pride wants to make us look after number one. Lord, please grant us humility, which is the mother of all virtue, so that we can live together in harmony as Your children. In Jesus' name we pray. Amen! :)

July 17

Father God, thank You for our inclination towards righteousness. Whether we admit it or not, we are miserable when we sin. When we sin, we are constantly anxious to make sure no one finds out. When we sin, we are scared that we will one day pay for our sins, either in this life or in the life to come. When we sin, we break relationships and hurt our loved ones and end up living alone. When we sin, we toss and turn in our sleep, haunted by our conscience, knowing that we did wrong. If we are falsely accused of wrong doing, we can rest assured that we didn't do anything wrong. If we choose not to cheat and do poorly on an exam, we can be assured that we did our best and left the rest up to You. If we treat everyone with love and kindness, we can enjoy the peace and friendship that comes with such actions. Lord, only when we are walking down the path of righteousness that we can truly be happy, no matter what happens in life. In Your name we pray. Amen! :)

What sin has made you miserable lately? How can you live a life without sin so that nothing weighs down your heart?

July 18

Dear God, thank You for entrusting to us all that You've blessed us with. Just like children who use their father's money to buy something for their dad, we never really give anything to You that never belonged to You in the first place. It is only until then that we can hold onto our blessings loosely. These blessings are not necessarily only material goods but also talents and skills that can be used for Your greater glory. Everything that we have was given to us, but they can also be easily taken away. When we base our happiness on that which cannot be taken away, namely You, then nothing that may happen to us can surely steal our joy. We have a transient mentality, that everything present is here today, and gone tomorrow. We are only on this rock momentarily, but we will spend eternity with You in heaven. But in the meantime, You've entrusted all things to us to be good stewards of Your creation. In Your precious name we pray. Amen! :)

What is your relationship with your blessings like? Do you hold onto your possessions loosely? How do you treat your time, talent and treasure?

July 19

Father God, thank You for building good character in us. Good character is doing the right thing even when no one is watching. It's being faithful with what we've been entrusted with even if we won't get caught doing wrong. It's living life knowing that You are watching our every move and that it makes You smile when You see us do as we ought to do. We know that Your Son will come one day unexpectedly to judge the living and the dead and we hope to be living righteously when He does so. We also know that our days are numbered and life will one day come to an end, so we put forth an effort to make the most of our limited time on earth, depositing into our spiritual bank accounts and investing in that which cannot fade away. Lord, may we recommit our hearts to You each and every day so that we do not get distracted by this world and continue to walk down the path of righteousness as we build good character. In Your precious name we pray. Amen! :)

How has your character been like lately? How can you build more character?

July 20
Dear God, thank You for humble hearts. We
know that humility is the mother of all virtue
and when we exercise that spiritual muscle, it
will get stronger. If there is anything that
pleases You most, it is a humble heart that
seeks to serve You in all that we do. In order to
adequately serve You, we must have the right
disposition of heart so that we can obey Your
commandments. And Your commandments are
others-centered rather than self-centered. You
constantly instruct us to love our neighbors as
we love ourselves. You want us to care for the
poor and needy, not be greedy and hoard all the
resources. You want us to swallow our pride if it
means preserving peace in the household. You
want wives to submit to the leadership of their
husbands, even if they desire to do something
else. Lord, may we humble ourselves today and
every day, for that honors You and is pleasing in
Your sight. In Your precious name we pray.
Amen! :)

How humble have you been lately? How
can you be more humble in your life?

180

Father God, thank You for boldness to stand for truth. In a society where truth is becoming "relative" and everyone is somehow right at the same time, we need to be more firm and resilient in protecting Your Word. The thing about truth is that it is not dependent on what people think and how many people believe it to be true; it's truth no matter what, and we must be keen to discern what is truth and what is not. Even if the whole world believed the world to be flat, it is still round; even if the whole world does not believe in gravity, people will still fall if they jump off an airplane. The truth still holds even when it's not the popular belief. The same applies in the area of sin; a sin is a sin no matter how dressed up or pretty it is. And it's up to us to boldly proclaim it to the world even if we're the only ones saying it. Lord, help us to be Your bearers of truth, not wavering when we face opposition but rather display even more humble boldness. In Your name we pray. Amen! :)

What truth has been recently jeopardized by our culture? What can you do to proclaim the truth in your life?

July 22

Father God, thank You for the challenges of life. Just like how a movie is interesting if something somehow goes wrong, challenges in our own lives keep our lives interesting. This journey called life is not a boring one but one that keeps us on our toes, not knowing what comes next but trusting that You have everything under control. Just like how Mary was put in a difficult situation, becoming pregnant out of wedlock, she probably felt like she was between a rock and a hard place. She probably never imagined her life to be the way it turned out- but she trusted You every step of the way. And she may have been tempted to feel that You have abandoned her simply because she was in her particular difficult situation, but it's when we hit rock bottom that we seek You most. Lord, may we not lose sight of You when we go through our twists and turns of life and try to enjoy the ride, trusting that You have conquered all. In Your name we pray. Amen! :)

What challenge have you encountered lately that has made your life a bit more interesting? How can you trust God with that new challenge?

July 23

Father God, thank You for second chances. As humans, we are bound to mess up. Our mistakes can be as grave as mortal sins or as small as venial sins, but both kinds of sins have the capacity to make us stray away from the path You have laid out for us. Just like the prodigal son indulged himself in all kinds of mortal sin and foolishness, and got himself into all kinds of trouble, You didn't focus on all that he did wrong, but You emphasized on all that he did right- and that was his decision to come back to his father. His realization of his mistakes in life came after a long series of consequences when a famine came by- but his father restored his position as his son even though he didn't necessarily deserve it. Lord, may we remember this beautiful parable when we ever feel that we are too far gone and not deserving of Your loving forgiveness. And may we share that same message of love with our lost family and friends so that they can come back to Your embrace. In Your name we pray. Amen! :)

What second chances have you been granted in your life? How have they impacted your life?

July 24

Father God, thank You for true friends. True friends are not just acquaintances or people that we know but people who are there for us through thick and thin. True friends not only know the pretty things about our lives but also the ugly- and still love us regardless. True friends are people that will tell you the truth even if it's difficult to hear, because they care for our well-being and desire to see change. True friends will pray for us even if we are resistant and don't want their prayers. A true friend is someone we can call in the middle of the night in the case of an emergency- and they will actually pick up to help. True friendship will stand the test of time and distance, for no matter how much time passes or how far away life drives 2 friends, true friendship will pick up from wherever it was left off. Lord, thank You for being the epitome of true friendship, loving us even as sinners. May we be true friends to our neighbors and embrace any true friends that You have blessed us with. In Your name we pray. Amen! :)

What qualities does a true friendship have? How have your true friends impacted your life?

Dear God, thank You for Your unifying Spirit. In a world where sin is rampant, we've learned quickly to put up walls. The walls we build not only protect us from any evil intention others may have but they also separate us from friends. The walls we build are numerous but weak rather than strong when collaborated with our neighbor to keep evil out and at bay. The walls we build keep a kingdom divided which will eventually fall in the face of disaster; but the bridges that we build enables for help to easily reach us. The bridges that we build helps us to collaborate and fend off evil together- with focused attention and intensity. Together we are strong and separated we will fall- because everyone has a unique gift that may not make sense individually but together it fits perfectly like a puzzle piece. Lord, may we not focus on our differences that result in building walls, but rather focus on how those differences make a unifying entity. In Your name we pray. Amen! :)

What walls have you put up lately? How can they be turned to bridges instead?

Father God, thank You for a generous heart. Contrary to our earthly kingdom, the economy of Your heavenly kingdom works quite different: those who try to save their lives will lose it and those who lose their lives for Your sake will save it. On the same note, those who give will receive, even 100-fold, for a hand that cannot open to give is not ready to receive because it's clenched so tight in fear that there will not be enough to share. Though it's not a sin to be rich, it surely comes with greater responsibility- a responsibility to tend to the needs of the poor and to give generously. Ironically, those who have much tend to give less and spend more on themselves but those who have less tend to give more and less on themselves. The art of giving shifts the focus off of ourselves and puts the attention on others. We were never meant to be selfish but others-centered, for self-centeredness is the quickest way to depression. Lord, may we have generous hearts that will freely tend to the needs of the poor so that we function as one family. In Your name we pray. Amen! :)

What is your understanding of God's counterintuitive economy? How has being others-centered brought you more happiness and joy than being self-centered?

July 27

Dear God, thank You for Your life-giving Word. Often times we believe that Your Word and statutes restrict our freedom; however, it was really meant to liberate us. Boundaries may seem like they wall us in, but really they keep us safe to better reach our goals. Your commandments may seem like they prevent us from living our lives and having the most fun possible, but rather they guide us down the path to have the best life possible. Your commandments may not make sense to us now as mere children, but they will make sense later when we can look back and see how Your guidance have helped us dodge the schemes of the evil one. Your commands may seem counterintuitive and contrary to our natural tendencies, but we will later realize that it is the sinful flesh that we have to put to death in order for our spirits to flourish. Lord, grant us abiding spirits seeking to obey Your Word even when we don't understand it, for we know it is life-giving. In Your name we pray. Amen! :)

How has the Word been life-giving to you?

July 28

Father God, thank You for being fully devoted. With just a quick glance around, it's evident that today's society has bred half-hearted investments. With too much going on, our attentions tend to be divided, and nothing gets our full attention. With social media advertising thousands of friends, and yet we fail to build real, deep friendships. We are satisfied with simply knowing "of" You, but never take the time to get to "know" You. As with anything that is worth pursuing, it takes time and persistence but the blessings that are reaped with intentional and full-hearted devotion can last a life time and even eternity. Lord, may we model after Your unconditional love for us so that we exemplify that love back to You and our neighbors. In Jesus' precious name we pray. Amen! :)

Have you been fully devoted? How can you be more focused on what is most important?

July 29

Father God, thank You for a world without borders. It doesn't take long for one to realize that as broken human beings, we quickly build up walls to separate us from our neighbor. As broken human beings, we try to make one race superior to another, even though You created us equal. As broken human beings, we tend to reserve our love and compassion to those that we care for, even though You commanded us to care for everyone, regardless of background. But You didn't want to leave us "broken" and gave Your life so that we can become more righteous. You command us to not only love our friends but also our enemies, so that one day they may become our friends. You command us to treat others the way we would like to be treated, so that we can come to care for each other the way we were intended to care. You command us to love our neighbor and tend to their needs, even to the point of risking our own lives and safety, for that is the ultimate sign of love. Lord, may we look past the walls we built and see our neighbors as people to love. In Your name we pray. Amen! :)

How can you help create a world without borders?

189

July 30

Dear God, thank You for wisdom and prudence. Prudence is the ability to govern and discipline oneself by the use of reason. Prudence is the practice of predicting what the future may hold and changing course if the path leads to sin. Prudence is preparing for the storm even before the storm comes. Prudence is seeing the good habits of righteous people and emulating them in hopes of becoming good and righteous like them. A prudent man leads his heart rather than blindly following his heart, so that both his heart and his mind can come to agreement and end up somewhere desirable. At the end of the day, although we are all dealt with a different hand of cards, life is what we make it- and success is when preparation meets opportunity. Lord, may we lead prudent lives, seeking Your wisdom to keep us rooted, avoiding sin and striving to be all that You created us to be. In Your name we pray. Amen! :)

How have you been prudent in your life lately? In what ways can you be more prudent?

Father God, thank You for neighbors. Although a neighbor can be cruel and indifferent, a good neighbor would be compassionate and kind, treating their neighbors the way they would like to be treated. It's easy to get comfortable and shut out the rest of the world when we are fine and lack nothing- but we are called to see how we can help those in need. There will always be need in this broken world- physical, spiritual, emotional, financial, etc.- that we can never say that there is no way to help. A neighbor does not necessarily have to be someone that lives next door but may be someone in another lower income community; a neighbor may not look or think like us but live in an entirely different country with an entirely different culture; we may even address the needs of homeless and hungry animals that need help in the face of devastation. The ways to use our time, talent and treasure to help another in need is endless- we just have to seek and seize the opportunities. Lord, may we be Your hands and feet as we help those around us in any way we can after devastation strikes. In Your name we pray. Amen! :)

What are some needs that need to be addressed in your community? What about around the nation? How about around the world?

August 1

Father God, thank You for spiritual health. Spiritual health is the gauge that measures the closeness of our relationship with You. It's the path to inner peace that we can experience despite the turmoil that may be happening around us. Spiritual health is the ability to be joyful when irritable things don't irritate us anymore. It's the ability to be grateful for everything, taking the good in with the bad. Spiritual health is being happy even when things don't go our way, for rarely they ever do. Spiritual health is being focused on the mission given to us and not being distracted by menial or worldly things. Along with physical, emotional and mental health, spiritual health is a very important part of life that must be nourished and maintained by constant fellowship with You, our Creator. Lord, may we dedicate the time and energy necessary to nurture our relationship with You so that our spiritual health would flourish. In Your name we pray. Amen! :)

How is your spiritual health? Do you find yourself more irritated than not? How can you strengthen your spiritual health?

August 2

Father God, thank You for gratitude. We were
created to be grateful and when we are not, we
fall victim to vices such as discontentment,
dissatisfaction and pride. There may be a
hundred reasons why we should be sad and
unhappy in this broken world, but there are
thousands of reasons why we should not, but
rather joyful and happy. Sure, there is hatred
and war and poverty and hunger, but there is
also love, and peace and prosperity and
abundance- in fact, there is enough to go
around and still have plenty left over- we just
have to do our part and share. Your Word even
instructs us to be happy in everything, giving
You praise for the good AND the bad. It makes
us shift our perspective to see the glass full and
not empty, even when we're tempted to complain
about not having the glass entirely full. Not
complaining gets even more difficult when our
neighbors seemingly have more than us- then we
get even more ungrateful for what You have
already blessed us with. But we must realize
that You are God and we are not, and we have
no say regarding Your generosity- You have
every right to be generous with whomever You
so desire, and we should be grateful for that.
Lord, may we cultivate grateful hearts to see
the blessings in this world so that we can bring
You our utmost praise. In Your name we pray.
Amen! :)

Do you tend to be happy in the good AND
the bad? How can we refrain from
complaining and focus on our blessings?

August 3

Father God, thank You for a clean heart. In this superficial world, everyone is concerned with the outside and how things appear; but You are more concerned about what's happening on the inside. Yes, it's important to be physically clean for hygienic purposes but You call us to be spiritually clean as well, for moralistic purposes. A heart that is moral has nothing to worry about because it is in right standing with You, our ultimate judge. A heart that is moral can sleep at night for it knows it has done nothing wrong and is not afraid of being caught and reprimanded. A heart that is moral can be at peace for it knows that it not only refrained from evil but also committed to doing good for others. A heart that is moral can look back on its life and see a positive change in the world, simply because they existed and were proactive. Lord, may we develop good character that commits to doing good even when no one is looking so that we can cultivate a pure and clean heart that is in right standing with you. In Your precious name we pray. Amen! :)

Have you been cultivating a clean heart?
How can you continue to live a clean life?

"Create in me a pure heart, O God,
and renew a steadfast spirit within me." -Psalm 51:10

Father God, thank You for good character. Good character is doing good even when not noticed or recognized. Just like how You tell us to not boast of our good deeds, preventing the right hand from knowing what the left hand has done, You tell us to continue to do good for Your name's sake and for Your greater glory. Yes, it gets difficult when we faithfully do our job, do our part and receive no credit for it; but we know that You, our Father sees everything and we can rest assured that our actions are being noticed, by You if not by man. Good character is the tendency to continue to perform despite the difficult situations that may be surrounding- trusting that one day our good character will shine for itself without us ever having to say anything. Father God, may we continue to embrace the practice of doing our very best in everything that we are entrusted to do to develop good character and bring You glory with our lives. In Your precious name we pray. Amen!

:)

How has your character been developing lately? Do you feel unnoticed sometimes for your good works?

August 5

Father God, thank You for death. Although our society pretends that death doesn't exist and tries to escape the inevitable, You allow death to happen so that we can realize that our days are numbered. Life is a gift that You have given to us out of love, but often times we misuse it. We act as if our lives were meant to be all about us and we tend to forget about others. We live as if we would never die, and then when it comes to dying, we die as if we never lived-holding onto any string of life that we can get. We get caught up in little minor details that we blow up into major problems and forget the frailty of life. We use our intelligence to create atomic bombs and destroy our neighbors in war. Lord, help us to cherish and embrace every moment that You have given us, for we know that life is a gift and death is just another step in life to get closer to You. In Your name we pray. Amen! :)

What is your relationship with death like? Do you acknowledge the frailty of life and appreciate every moment?

August 6

Father God, thank You for humility. Humility is the virtue that reminds us that everything that we have is a gift and we are not entitled to anything more. Humility is the art of thinking of others before ourselves, keeping the focus of life in right perspective. Humility is the appreciation of every little detail of life, finding beauty in everything. Humility is not feeling superior or inferior to another, just each other's equal, standing side-by-side as brothers and sisters in Christ. Lord, may we embrace the virtue of humility today and every day, so that we can grow in appreciation for all that You have already blessed us with. In Your name we pray. Amen! :)

What is the role of humility in your life? Do you treat others with humility?

August 7

Father God, thank You for blessing us. Although we are very grateful for all that You have blessed us with, we know those blessings should not stop with us but make its way to others- for we are blessed to be a blessing. Often times we get so caught up with what's happening in our own lives, that we fail to see the need in our neighbors' lives. Often times we get so warped up in our "problems" and fail to realize that they're not problems at all when compared to the problems of the world. Often times we like to hoard all our blessings, not realizing that we're only hurting ourselves, for there is tremendous blessing in generosity. Lord, help us to seek for opportunities to share of our time, treasure and talent so that we can become more of the Christian community You desire of us. In Your precious name we pray. Amen! :)

How have you used your blessings to bless others lately? Have you shared as much as you think you should?

Father God, thank You for love. Love is an over-
used word that has eventually lost its powerful
meaning; but essentially, love is what everything
is about at the end of the day. You Yourself are
Love, who created us to love, so that we would
love You back as well as our neighbors. It is
through love that we commit our entire lives to
another human being in marriage to bring forth
yet another human being. It is through love
when we go the extra mile beyond our normal
duties in life to help another in need. Basically
everything that we do is looking for love- either
to love another or to be loved by another; but
of course, not everyone is looking for love in the
right places. The true source of love is from
You, who is the first one to essentially love us
into existence and continued to love us in our
sin. May we supply our need for love from Your
bountiful sources so that we can love others in
supernatural ways. Lord, help us to grasp
opportunities to express love in the many forms
that it comes in- bringing forth life in every
circumstance. In Your name we pray. Amen! :)

What is love in your life like? Are you
looking for love in the right places?

August 9

Father God, thank You for righteous guilt. Righteous guilt, unlike earthly guilt, brings life and not death. It is the shame that we feel that makes us stop in our tracks and turn around when we are sinning. It is the little voice in our head that is encouraging us to stop living a life of sin and to start anew in our walk towards You. It is a constant reminder that You are an all-forgiving Father that is waiting with arms spread wide to receive us yet once again. Lord, may we use any guilt that we feel not as a punishment but as a signal that nudges us to make changes in our lives that will bring forth fruit. In Your precious name we pray. Amen! :)

Have you experienced righteous guilt recently in your life? What was it like? Did it push you in the right direction?

Father God, thank You for prayer. Prayer is the gift of communication that we have with You, our Creator. Prayer is not dependent on any technology and is not confined to time and space but is a supernatural form of communication that can transcend even spiritual dimensions. It's the lifeline You bless us with to stay connected throughout our day. Often times when our lives get "busy", we tend to cut back on our prayer life. We find urgent things to be more important than spending quality time with You. But the "tyranny of the urgent" will eventually reveal that the urgent things are not usually the important things in life. It's the "not so urgent" things in life that are more important but tend to get pushed to the wayside simply because they are not urgent. But as history reveals, behind every good man, woman, family or community is a prayer warrior or giant, praying for everyone's needs- may we be that prayer warrior/giant in our circle of influence today. Lord, help us to take the time and effort to nourish our prayer time with You- whatever it may look like, during the morning, at night, during lunch, throughout the day, etc.- and make it a priority in our lives, for we know it's our lifeline. In Your precious name we pray. Amen! :)

What is your prayer life like? How has the "urgent" in your life tried to take your attention from prayer?

August 11

Father God, thank You for Your sacrifice. You did the unthinkable and came down from heaven, became man, confined to restrictions of time and space and normal human limitations, and suffered a gruesome death for our sake so that we may have everlasting life with You. You died to take away the sin of the world for sin is detestable in Your sight. To live in sin is to be miserable, but we are so weak that we continue to fall into our earthly desires. Though the spirit may be willing, the flesh is weak, but through Your sacrifice on the cross 2000 years ago, we have what it takes to overcome sin. Though it may not be easy, You have given us the Holy Spirit, which enables us to live in righteousness, supporting us every step of the way. Righteousness is not attained in a single moment but a lifetime of surrender and commitment to doing Your will. Lord, help us to remember that You have given us the ability to overcome sin and may we use that divine power to live in righteousness. May we take time from our busy schedules to reflect on areas in our lives that need to be purified and purged of all sin. In Your beautiful name we pray. Amen! :)

Do you recognize God's sacrifice in your life? How has it empowered you to live and strive for holiness?

Father God, thank You for Your goodness and grace. You truly want to bless us and have the best in mind for us. We just have to exercise the ability to trust You in all Your ways. We tend to grow impatient, thinking that You have not heard our prayers if they're not answered in the way we think they should be answered. We have not realized that answers to our prayers can be a "yes", a "no", or a "not now". The only time that we think our prayers have been answered is when it's a "yes". But God wants what's best for us and we have to trust Him when the answer we receive is "no" or "not now". When the answer is "no", He's really saying that He has something better in mind. And when He says "not now", we have to trust and be patient for God's perfect timing. Our good father in heaven cannot be outdone and as any good father, He will discipline us when needing to be disciplined and reward us when a reward is warranted. Lord, grant us strength to trust you and believe You in all Your promises of grace and goodness in our lives. In Jesus' mighty name, we pray. Amen! :)

Do you trust that God has your best in mind? Have you ever thought that God didn't answer your prayers when the answer was actually "no" or "not now"?

August 13

Father God, thank You for entrusting us with whatever You have entrusted to us. Though we know that what we have is temporary and will not be with us forever, we tend to cling to anything and everything we get our hands on. Though we know that everything that we have is not really ours but lent to us in the meantime, we tend to hoard and refuse to share what wasn't really ours in the first place. Though we work hard to make a living for our families, we fail to remember that You are the author of wealth and allow us to accumulate wealth in the first place. Lord, may we have a healthy relationship with the things You have blessed us with on earth, so that we can use them wisely in the meantime and depart from it when we have to, being generous with our time, talent and treasure. In Your name we pray. Amen! :)

What is your relationship like with what God has entrusted you during your time on earth? Do you feel you have a divine responsibility to use those blessings wisely?

Father God, thank You for Your 2nd coming. Although we don't know exactly when You are coming back, we just know You said You will return to judge the living and the dead. This return is frightening for the evildoer but refreshing for the righteous one committed to doing Your will. This return is the end for all evil but the beginning of everlasting peace and joy. This return resembles the return of the groom in ancient times coming back for his bride- where You are coming back to pick up Your Bride, the Church. Lord, may we be mindful of Your second coming and not become complacent in these lives we lead- but rather alert and ready to wage war on evil. In Your name we pray. Amen! :)

How has Jesus' promised 2nd coming encouraged you to keep moving forward in your walk of life? Does it encourage you to not look back?

August 15

Dear God, thank You for gratitude. Gratitude is the art of being grateful and appreciative for anything and everything. Gratitude is not dependent on external circumstances but can be exercised no matter the situation. Gratitude is not dependent on financial or material possessions but can be exercised with the least of things. Gratitude is not dependent on simply the good that happens to us but can also be implemented with the bad, soaking in Your wonderful atoning sacrifice 2000 years ago, granting us future grace in which we can hope for. It's about time that we develop and maintain attitudes of gratitude, not just on a specific day of the year but year-round. Lord, help us to focus on something to be grateful for each and every day, pouring out our praise to You, the provider of every good thing. In Your name we pray. Amen! :)

What are you grateful for today? Do you struggle with being grateful each day? What can you do today to help you cultivate an attitude of gratitude?

August 16

Father God, thank You for joy. Joy is the
inherent sense of peace and contentment
despite the surrounding circumstances. Unlike
our society, which promises fleeting "happiness",
You promise us never-ending joy that's so deep
inside us that the enemy cannot get to. Unlike
our society, which insists on finding happiness in
people, places and things, You show us how
happiness is found within us and not around us.
Unlike our society, which creates a restless
culture of trying to find happiness, You teach us
to find happiness in stillness and simplicity. Lord,
may we not settle for happiness that is not
ever-satisfying but strive to attain the joy that
is found within, which is sustained by our
relationship with You. In Your name we pray.
Amen! :)

In what ways have you found joy in your
life? Was it in stillness and simplicity?

August 17

Father God, thank You for Your mercy. Mercy is sparing us from what we really deserve. As mere humans, we are inclined to sin, even though we have every intention not to. We know that the punishment for sin is death, and we are eternally grateful for Your sacrifice giving us new life, even when we were still sinners. And we know that You are aware of our tendency to sin, granting us grace to be able to overcome sin with Your divine power. We know that it's not when we sin that makes You sad, but when we don't actively do anything about our sin, bringing them to the foot of the cross and laying them down at Your feet. We know that it's when we become comfortable and complacent with our sin that makes You most sad. And for that very reason, we wake up each morning with a renewed sense of purpose, with every intention to combat sin and the schemes of the devil with the power of Your Holy Spirit. Lord, help us to identify the sin in our lives that need to be eradicated and removed in order to be holy and pleasing in Your sight. In Your merciful name we pray. Amen! :)

When was a recent time that you sinned and got back up? Did you feel God's mercy in that experience?

August 18

Father God, thank You for silence. It is in the silence that we can take a moment and self-reflect, identifying areas of our hearts that need healing and sin that needs to be removed. It is in the silence that we can stop and take our bearings, reorienting ourselves to go in the direction we wish to go. It is in the silence that we can hear Your voice more clearly, away from the chaos and distraction of the world outside. In a culture that tries to fill in every moment of silence with noise, we must be more vigilant to preserve silence and moments of peace. Lord, may we appreciate moments of silence in our lives as opportunities to connect with You, drawing evermore closer to You. In Your precious name we pray. Amen! :)

How have moments of silence helped you gain direction and self-reflect? Do you actively seek these moments of silence?

Father God, thank You for Your healing. It doesn't take long for us to get acquainted with pain in this life; life is more like a battleship rather than a cruise ship and we must be ready for war. But when we have taken a beating and suffered so much pain, we seek Your face for healing and restoration of our souls to go back out into the battlefield. And though it is ultimately through You that grants us the complete healing, You command us to do our part in tending to other people's wounds. You command us to forgive as it will be forgiven unto us. You teach us to love, as we were first loved by You. You instruct us to reconcile with our brothers and sisters, even before coming to You at the altar. You command us to never let the sun go down angry at our loved ones, in order to not give the evil one a foothold in our hearts. Lord, help us to do our part in stimulating the healing process in ourselves as well as in our neighbors. In Your sweet name we pray. Amen! :)

How have you done your part to facilitate healing in your life or someone else's life?

Father God, thank You for change. As we all know, the only constant in life is change, either for the better or for the worse. Whether we like it or not, we're constantly changing physically, emotionally and spiritually with every passing day- and it's up to us if we choose to become ever more closer to You or slowly slip away. We are never the same person as we were yesterday or will be tomorrow, for we gain new experiences that heavily or slightly influence our beings in every which way. We are not the same person as we were when we were children, for now we are adults with adult responsibilities- and possibly little ones to take care of. The people around us are not the same people they were in the past for they too are on their own journey, being molded into whatever they choose to be molded. Lord, we know that change is inevitable but help us to embrace change, for better or for worse, and allow us to grow as a person with every new experience. In Jesus' name we pray. Amen! :)

What is your relationship with change? Do you welcome it or do you avoid it?

August 21

Father God, thank You for commitment. In this day and age, nothing is built to last, whereas everything in the past was built to last forever. As a result, when something is broken, the first thought that comes to mind is to toss and replace it, rather than fix it. Unfortunately, this has seeped into relationships and marriages, where relationships have become dispensable and marriage vows hold no weight. But we believe Your words when You said, what You bind together and counted as one, let no man separate. Sure, commitment is difficult but it's worth it in the end. Sure, commitment is tough, but so is non-commitment where many other sins and vices enter due to the non-commitment. Sure, commitment is challenging but so is everything else in life that is worth pursuing. Lord, may we counteract the culture of non-commitment and keep our word, especially the promise of forever in marriage. In Your name we pray. Amen! :)

What is your relationship with commitment like? Are you able to commit to something that is worth committing?

August 22

Father God, thank You for Your faithfulness. Often times, we go about our lives feeling that we're alone and that we have to fend for ourselves. We forget that You are our loving Father and want what is best for us, if only that we ask. We tend to put our trust in man when disaster strikes, but forget that You are the Father Almighty, who is capable of doing miracles and wonders. We tend to get anxious trying to control a situation, forgetting that You are ultimately in control of everything. We tend to manage our problems on our own, thinking that You have other more important problems to deal with in the world, but forget that You are God and are not confined by human limitations.

Lord, help us to swim in Your faithfulness, trusting You in all that we do, so that we don't drown in our doubts. In Your precious name we pray. Amen! :)

Do you have faith in God's faithfulness? Do you trust that He is in control? How can you rest more in His faithfulness?

August 23

Dear God, thank You for being our good Father. As our Heavenly Father, You desire what's best for us and as Your earthly children, we have to heed to Your discipline, even when we don't like it. There will be times that we don't understand our circumstances and why we have to deal with them. There will be times when we would rather be lost and isolated from our community of faith but we know it's best to stay connected. There will be times that we feel You are silent and distant, but we know that You are always there, even when we don't feel you. As our Good Father, You sent Your Son as our Good Shepherd, to clearly demonstrate the love You have for us, that You would lay down Your life for Your sheep. As our Good Father, You desire that no one be lost, but that they would be searched for day and night until they are safe and back in the fold. Lord, may we be comforted to depend on You as our Good Father, who desires the best for us as Your feeble children. In Your mighty name, we pray. Amen! :)

Do you see God as a Good Father? How has He been a Good Father in your life?

Father God, thank You for Your generosity. As mere humans, we find it unfair when You show such wonderful generosity to others and we are blessed with what's sufficient. It's not difficult to realize that we don't need much to be happy in this life, but we tend to make ourselves unhappy when You seem to bless others more than us. It's quite clear to us that we have everything that we need, yet we tend to desire more. We know that You are the source of every good thing, and that when we have a good relationship with You, we have everything, but we tend to forget and get distracted by what's shiny on the other side. Lord, help us to be satisfied with what You have blessed us with and not get jealous when You show favor to our neighbor. In Your precious name we pray. Amen!

:)

How do you respond when it seems that God has blessed others more than you? Do you get jealous or do you praise God for His generosity?

Father God, thank You for wisdom. Wisdom is the art of putting into practice good habits and actions. It is not enough to "know" what's good to do, but to actually execute the good actions- for that is when wisdom is vindicated. It is not enough to tell others what to do, but rather to lead by example, for that is the ultimate way to influence those around us. It is not enough to wish to do something, for then wisdom gets stuck in the desire stage and nothing gets done, especially in a world of great and dire need. Lord, we know that the wisdom of this world is folly in Your eyes- please bless us with Your heavenly wisdom, so that we may live out good and godly lives, for Your greater glory. In Your precious name we pray. Amen! :)

How has wisdom been active in your life? Do you *know* what's good and actually do it?

Father God, thank You for serenity. Serenity is the practice of being calm and serene, even in the midst of chaos. It doesn't take long for us to realize that this world is not perfect and the people inhabiting the world is even more broken. All this is evidence that we are in dire need of a savior, to save us from all of our sin and the devastation of the world. But what we fail to realize is that we can still experience Your inexplicable peace even in the sea of turmoil. We can still experience a calming of our spirit when we conjoin with Your Spirit, even when the world is upside down and crazy. We can still experience clarity, even in the ocean of confusion, as long as we keep our eyes fixated on You. Lord, we can't control our circumstances but we can surrender our thoughts and actions to You, allowing You to lead us down the path of righteousness and peace. In Your sweet name we pray. Amen! :)

When was the last time you experienced true serenity and peace in the midst of chaos in your life?

August 27

Father God, thank You for actions. As we all know, action speaks louder than words. It's not enough to say that we will do something and not follow through. It's not enough to have good intentions for even the best intentions may fall short and result in devastation. It's not enough to make promises, especially when we don't have the capacity to fulfill those promises or even have the intentions to do so. Though You like to examine the heart, we know that at the end of the day, it's what we actually do that really matters. We know that the spirit is willing but the flesh is weak, and we need Your help to obey Your commandments. Lord, help us to abide in Your Word and do what is holy and pleasing in Your sight. In Your precious name we pray. Amen! :)

Do you ever find yourself making empty promises? Do you follow through with your words? Make an effort today to make your *yes* be *yes* and your *no* be *no*.

August 28

Father God, thank You for gifts. Gifts are an outward expression of an inward disposition of gratitude and joy. They are physical manifestations of the happiness that we feel towards another during a special occasion or any random day. But often times we lose the sight of the purpose of a gift. We tend to expect gifts when we really shouldn't. We tend to become bitter when a gift is not as we expected. We tend to place our worth in the value of the gift received, rather than soaking up the invaluable gift You blessed us with 2000 years ago. Lord, help us to focus on what's really important in the art of gift-giving, having the right perspective when we practice this beautiful art. In Your name we pray. Amen! :)

What is your relationship with gift giving? Do you love to give gifts? Receive gifts? Have you or someone you know ever received a gift but were disappointed? What can you learn from that experience?

August 29

Father God, thank You for simplicity. Often times, we think that more is better, especially in this consumeristic society. But if we allow ourselves to objectively observe, we come to realize that sometimes less is best. When we find that our joy and happiness is not rooted in material things or things to do, but in a relationship with You, our Creator, we find ourselves finding satisfaction in the place that we are. We stop coveting what our neighbor has and start desiring what we have already been blessed with. We stop looking for more, for we realize we have all that we need. We stop trying to do it all, for we know that being "present" wherever we are is the greatest joy and gift we can ever give ourselves. Lord, may we learn to be more satisfied with what You have already blessed us with and not strive for more, because more is not always better. In Your precious name we pray. Amen! :)

How has simplicity been a blessing in your life? Are you able to see past all the fluff of more?

Father God, thank You for Your presence. As we all know, one of the most valuable thing anyone can possess is time. Time for many people is the most restrictive resource to any project in mind. Because it is so limited, and we do not have the power to grant ourselves more time, wherever we choose to spend the time that we do have demonstrates the value that we place in that particular area of our lives. Although we all are blessed with the same amount of time, some people will never *"have the time"* to spend with family and loved ones. Although no one has more time than another, some people will never *"have the time"* to take care of the poor and needy. Although there are 24 hours in a day and 7 days in a week around the world, many people will not *"have the time"* to spend at least one hour with You on Sunday. At the end of the day, it's not about not "*having the time*" but rather "*making the time*" for things that are important and are prioritized over trivial things. You understand the importance of being present with Your people and decided to *"take the time"* to come down from Your throne in heaven and be with us- Emmanuel. Lord, help us to prioritize our lives so that we can make the time to be present in places that are most important. In Your name we pray. Amen! :)

What important aspect of your life do you *"not have the time"* to do? How can you *"make the time"*?

Father God, thank You for doing the impossible. In a world that is so limited and restricted, we tend to develop attitudes of despair. We become hopeless when we encounter troubles in our lives, disregarding the numerous times You have intervened and performed a miracle. It is for the very reason of our forgetfulness that You institute certain monuments and feast days to remind us of Your faithfulness. When medical science informs us that we only have a certain time to live, You say otherwise- because ultimately You are the one who numbers our days. When our wombs are barren and cannot bring forth children, You surprise us with a beautiful bundle of joy, but of course in Your perfect timing. When we yearn for countless years for someone to love and have given up on that dream, You unexpectedly throw us in the path of someone that we will spend the rest of our lives with, and we may never have seen it coming. In a world of uncertainty, we can be certain of Your faithfulness. Lord, help us to remember that You are God and have the ability to do the impossible- we just have to trust and believe. In Jesus' mighty name we pray. Amen! :)

What "*impossible*" aspect of your life have you given up on? Do you believe that God can do the impossible?

September 1

Father God, thank You for perspective. To every story, there are multiple different angles and perspectives. Just like a picture that is snapped in one angle may portray the moment in a beautiful way, a picture that is snapped in a different angle may, on the other hand, poorly capture the moment and portray it in a bad light. We must remember that any object of attention, no matter how good or bad, can be portrayed in a positive light or a negative light. So is the case with what happens in our own lives- something can be a blessing or a curse, depending on how we perceive it. Singleness can be a great opportunity to serve You and others and build up towards our future or a time of severe loneliness. Challenges can be an opportunity for growth and development of character, or a time we get downtrodden and depressed. Minor annoyances can be opportunities to overlook for the sake of the overall good or be blown entirely out of proportion and exaggerated. Lord, help us to maintain the right perspective in everything that You bring into our lives, whether good or bad, and may we see the good that can come out of the bad. In Your name we pray. Amen! :)

Do you tend to see what happens in your life in a positive or negative perspective? How can you see your life more in a positive light?

Father God, thank You for experience. Despite what young people think, our elders tend to know more and are wiser simply because they've experienced more. It is through our pride and arrogance as children that we believe we know better than our elders and insist on doing things our own way. But that ideology comes with its own pitfalls, though it's disguised as "freedom." Making it on our own and disregarding the advice of our elders tends to result in making the same mistakes of our elders, rather than learning from their mistakes. Trying to pave our own path often results in us reinventing the wheel rather than building off of what our elders already discovered. Trying to find our own way through life often tends to result in going in circles and even backwards, rather than heeding to the advice of our elders and progressing from that. While our culture teaches us to "live and learn", You teach us to "learn and live", learning from the experience of our elders so that we can *live* to our greatest potential. Lord, help us to see the jewels of wisdom our elders hold and may we apply to our own lives what we learn from their experience. In Your name we pray. Amen! :)

_____

What have you learned from an elder recently? Do you tend to *live and learn* or *learn and live?*

September 3

Father God, thank You for the outsiders.
Outsiders are the people of any exclusive group.
You chose the people of Israel to be Your
exclusive children but it was all part of a plan.
The nation of Israel was chosen to demonstrate
to the rest of the world of Your unfailing love,
but You still had everyone else in mind. You
have chosen us to be the Body of Christ but
only to be the hands and feet that reaches out
to the world in need. You have chosen us to be
blessed with certain attributes, but only to be a
blessing to those that are lacking and need our
love and attention. Exclusivity is a good thing,
but only with the intention of bringing the
blessings to everyone else. Lord, help us to
reach out to the outsiders in our lives, for it's
the outsiders that You are most concerned
about. In Your name we pray. Amen! :)

How have you reached out to the people
on the outside recently?

September 4

Father God, thank You for the little things. Little things are the small trivial aspects of our lives that we easily take for granted or don't see as significant. Quite often, we set our eyes for the big goal ahead, but forget to take the time to enjoy the small blessings we have each day. Quite often, we believe that we have to do something big in the world to make a difference, but forget that You can use even the smallest act of kindness to touch a person's heart and create something beautiful. Quite often, we feel like we have to make strong and bold comments to get a message across, but forget that sometimes the strongest messages in life are made without words. Lord, may we have the eyes to see how impactful the little things in life can be and be mindful to nurture them. In Your name we pray. Amen! :)

What little thing in your life have you taken for granted? Do you believe that God can take the smallest act and turn it into something beautiful and grand? How does that change your perspective of your life?

September 5

Father God, thank You for imperfections. Imperfections are simply shortcomings of an accepted standard. As a society, we learn to veer away from imperfections, covering up every blemish there is on our faces, hiding away any mistake we may have made, and undergoing multiple surgeries to achieve this idea of "perfection", which we seem to never attain. But we tend to forget that You don't expect perfection from us; however, You desire faithfulness, of which You can work with. As we take a look at the Holy Family, they were not "perfect" according to our standards, but they were faithful. The disciples were not "perfect" in our eyes, but they kept their eyes on You.

Your prophets did not fit our image of "perfection", but they proclaimed Your message with all of their hearts. Lord, may we embrace our "imperfections" and surrender them to You, allowing You to do Your miraculous work in us to make us perfect in Your eyes. In Your name we pray, amen! :)

What imperfections do you have that you tend to hide? How can that "*imperfection*" be used for God's glory?

September 6

Father God, thank You for witnesses. Witnessing is the practice of sharing what we personally saw and experienced. Witnessing about our relationship with You is sharing with our neighbors the impact and intimacy the relationship has on us. Witnessing does not only take place in a judge's courthouse or on the stand, but every day and with every minute. We witness with our actions when we demonstrate to people that a relationship with you changes us for the better. We witness with our words when we lift people up and direct them down the right path, instead of tearing people down and leading them astray. We witness with our finances, when we place our treasure where You would have us put it, reaching out to those in need and showing them that we care. Lord, may we always embrace the opportunities to witness to Your name and may we not falter when the time comes. In Your name we pray. Amen! :)

How have you witnessed with your life lately? Does your life speak of the wonderful and intimate relationship we share with our God?

September 7

Father God, thank You for the extraordinary. As we live day to day, the extraordinary becomes ordinary to us and we lose the awe it deserves. The mere fact that we are alive on this little rock called "earth" suspended in the nothingness of space should blow our minds- but it doesn't, and we live as if our existence is meaningless. The mere fact that You, our Creator, desired to become one with Your creation and became man 2000 years ago should be incomprehensible to us- but it's not, as we celebrate that glorious event without being fully aware of the reason for the season. The mere fact that Your Son walked this earth, suffered death and rose again on the 3rd day should be unfathomable and take our breaths away- but it doesn't and has become another holiday we celebrate without truly appreciating its value. Lord, help us to bring back the awe in our view of all that has happened in the past as well as all that happens today, fully appreciating the extraordinary for what it's worth. In Your name we pray. Amen! :)

What is something extraordinary in our lives have we been taking for granted? How can we change our views of that?

September 8

Father God, thank You for joy. Joy is that inner sense of contentment despite external circumstances. It doesn't take long for us to realize that things are not always going to go our way, but that doesn't mean that we cannot have joy in our hearts regardless. Illness can strike and take away our loved ones, but the hope of reuniting with them again rejuvenates that joy. The economy can crash and we lose our jobs, but our humility to seek help and reach out to family and loved ones strengthen the bonds we share and maintain the joy lit in our hearts. We may have planned our lives to go one way, and it ends up going another, but our trust in You allows us to relax and enjoy the ride, wherever it may lead us. Lord, we know that life is constantly changing and things may not always go according to plan, but help us to see the beauty in everything that happens, relying on You and nurturing our joy. In Your name we pray. Amen! :)

Have you been able to hold onto joy in the midst of changing times and difficult moments? How has hope played into that?

Father God, thank You for light. Light expels
the darkness and brings life. It is quite
apparent that our society tends to embrace the
darkness for darkness covers the reality of sin.
Though darkness may seem warm and cozy, it
hides the sorrow that comes with it. Though
darkness may be easy on the eyes, it slowly but
surely suffocates the life out of us. Though
darkness seems to be attractive and appealing,
it keeps us away from the true joy that comes
with light. But the good news is that, although
sorrow may last through the night, joy comes in
the morning, with the breaking of dawn. The
beauty of the rising sun is the reality of a new
day with new possibilities. All the limitations
that we faced yesterday does not have to be
the limitations that we face tomorrow- for light
reveals strengths that we never knew were
there. Disease result from the lack of exposure
to light, for light is healing with the proper
production of vitamins and the adequate
destruction of pathogens. Moreover, life results
from the proper exposure to light, nurturing
growth and vibrancy. Similarly, You are the
Light of the world, and Your children bear Your
light to the world for spiritual strength and
vitality. Lord, may we not hide Your light under
a bushel, but rather display it on a stand for all
the world to see. In Your name we pray. Amen!
:)

What is your relationship with light? Do
you tend to gravitate towards darkness?

Father God, thank You for words. Words are the combination of letters with assigned sounds that create syllables, which we can intelligently understand to communicate with one another. Although society teaches us that words are meaningless and cannot hurt, history and experience tell us otherwise. Words that come out of our mouths can either build up or tear down our neighbor, greatly impacting the course of their lives. Words can be used to sing You our praises and express the joy of our heart, or be full of curses, cursing You for putting us on this hard rock. Words can be passed down to record our history so that the younger generations can know the wonders You have done, or words can be manipulated to twist the truth so that no one can know the horrors that were done. Words spoken to ourselves can make the difference between success and failure, for whether we acknowledge it or not, we subconsciously assign a lot of value to words. Lord, help us to choose our words wisely, spoken to others, to You or to ourselves, for we know how powerful they can be and the lasting effects they can have. In Your mighty name we pray. Amen! :)

What is your relationship with words like? Do you use your words to build up or tear down others or yourself? How has other people's words impacted you in your life?

September 11

Father God, thank You for reminders. Essentially, reminders can be *anything* that remind us of something, either important or trivial. And reminders can take any shape or form, intentional or unintentional, yet still remind us of a certain truth. We place reminders of Your promises around us at home and at our jobs, committing them to memory so they can be abreast whenever we may need them. We institute certain days of the year to remind us to be thankful of our blessings at Thanksgiving, appreciate the love of our significant others at Valentine's Day, and show gratitude to our parents on Mothers'/Fathers' Day. We are shocked by the sudden death of a loved one and are reminded to seize and appreciate every moment, for we will never know when is the last. Lord, may we embrace every reminder, the easy ones and the difficult ones, for they remind us of what's really important in life. In Your name we pray, amen! :)

What reminders are important in your life? How have they reminded you of what's important?

September 12

Father God, thank You for doubt. Doubt is the skepticism that we face as feeble humans, questioning if something is really what we think it is. Our society breeds a culture of doubt, especially when it concerns You. As a result, there are swarms of people going astray and doing their own thing, never looking back. But You are not scared of doubt, for You are bigger than our silly questions. When we doubt, we tend to seek answers from others who may be older and wiser than we are, hoping that they can fill in some of the gaps. When we doubt, it shows that we are only human, with limited knowledge and understanding, of which is completed with faith. When we doubt, it drives us to seek truth, for we know that truth is absolute and not relative and it desires to be discovered. Lord, when we encounter doubt in our faith, may we not quiver in fear but approach it with boldness, giving us the resources that we need to find You in the end. In Your precious name we pray. Amen! :)

What is your relationship with doubt? Are you afraid of doubt? How has doubt strengthened your beliefs and brought you closer to God?

September 13

Father God, thank You for forgiveness.
Forgiveness is when we can create a clean slate
in a relationship so that we can move forward
without baggage. As we accumulate many years
in our lives, we tend to get bumps, bruises and
even scars along the way, but it is only when we
can forgive those who have hurt us, can we
really heal and move onto better and greater
things. Forgiveness is not only for the other
person but mostly for our sake. Forgiveness is so
counterintuitive and counter-cultural, but it's
the only way in Your Kingdom. Forgiveness is
easier to obtain when we realize how much
we've been forgiven. Lord, help us to forgive
others as You have forgiven us so that we can
nurture relationships that are holy and pleasing
to You. In Your mighty name we pray. Amen! :)

What is your relationship with forgiveness? Can
you forgive easily or do you take more time to
heal? How has forgiveness played out in your
life?

"And when you stand praying, if you hold anything against
anyone, forgive them, so that your Father in heaven may forgive
you your sins." – Mark 11:25

September 14

Father God, thank You for the ability to do good. Often times we find it sufficient to simply refrain from committing evil, but we fail to realize that not helping our brother and sister in need is bad in itself. We are not only expected to not steal from another but rather to bless others from the abundance of our hearts. We are not only expected to take care of ourselves and provide for our own natural needs, but rather cook and clean for those who cannot themselves. We are not only expected to pray for our own intentions but also the intentions of others, bringing our prayers to You so that they can be heard. Lord, although it is good to not do evil, but help us to seek opportunities to do good and bless others as You have blessed us. In Your name we pray, amen! :)

Do you find yourself taking an opportunity to do good whenever it comes your way? How can you do more good in your life?

Father God, thank You for the benefit of the doubt. In every situation, there are 2 sides of the story and we can choose to believe one or the other. Often times, the sides of the story are conflicting and one paints the situation in a better light than the other. Although our minds like to think ill of a situation, we ought to fight that temptation and pick the better of the two sides. Giving the benefit of the doubt helps maintain our relationship with our neighbors and makes our bonds stronger. Giving the benefit of the doubt helps us build positive energy and maintain a sound and peaceful mind. Giving the benefit of the doubt ultimately pleases You for we will think of what is holy, righteous, lovely, just, true, noble, pure, admirable, excellent and praiseworthy, leaving no room for anything else. Lord, though our spirit is willing, our flesh is weak and we ask that You would help us to see every situation in a positive light and give the benefit of the doubt when necessary. In Your precious name we pray. Amen! :)

Do you tend to give the benefit of the doubt? How does that practice help you to think of what's holy, righteous, lovely, just, true, noble, pure, admirable, excellent and praiseworthy?

Father God, thank You for "hypocrisy". We are all aware that church goers are often regarded as "hypocrites" because they don't necessarily always do as they preach. However, we often neglect the fact that they truly desire to do as they preach, and often fail because they are still human and struggle with sin. Fighting the flesh can be regarded as *doing the opposite of what we really want to do*, and can be seen as hypocrisy, but rather it's an active decision to do what is holy and pleasing in Your sight. "Hypocrisy" is when we tell others to love while we struggle to perfectly love, but still try to. "Hypocrisy" is when we don't feel like forgiving someone but we do because You first forgave us. "Hypocrisy" is when we give even when we don't want to, because we know You love an obedient heart, which then may eventually transform us into cheerful givers. Lord, may we not be discouraged when we fall into "hypocrisy" but rather fixate our eyes on You to help us fight against the flesh and be more like You. In Your name we pray. Amen! :)

When have you been regarded as a hypocrite when you failed to do to what you tend to preach to do? Do you acknowledge your shortcoming and continue to strive for holiness?

September 17

Father God, thank You for Your affirmation.

Affirmation is the action of testifying or declaring something to be true. In a world that constantly brings us down, we need Your Spirit to affirm us and keep us on solid ground. Your affirmation clarifies our identity in You and not in what we do. Your affirmation testifies that we are truly Your son and daughter and that we are beloved. Your affirmation enables us to see Your presence around us as You romance our hearts on a daily basis. Lord, may we not forget these undeniable truths but cling to them as they continue to affirm us in our everyday lives. In Your name we pray. Amen! :)

How has God affirmed you today? Do you feel like a daughter or son of the Most High? Do you feel God's presence in the world around you?

September 18

Father God, thank You for the ability to be hospitable. Hospitality is the act of friendliness and generosity towards guests and strangers. Although we live in a self-centered society which is always focused on receiving than giving, hospitality is a good practice to harbor in life. Hospitality towards our brothers and sisters opens the gate to love, especially when love is lacking in that relationship. Hospitality creates a generous and giving heart, which then makes us more grateful of the blessings You blessed us with. Hospitality towards everyone prevents discrimination against anyone- for we may be treating angels with kindness and respect and we won't even know it. Lord, create in us hospitable hearts so that we can share with others the over-abundance You've shared with us and ultimately create an atmosphere of love. In Your name we pray. Amen! :)

How have you been hospitable in your life recently? How was it a blessing to be hospitable to others?

September 19

Dear God, thank You for today. Today is the day of the present, and it's exclusive from yesterday and tomorrow. Our brains are advanced enough that it can keep track of yesterday, today and tomorrow- but sometimes it's best to just stay in the present. Often times, we get anxious of what tomorrow holds because all the kinks have not been ironed out yet, but that is why You didn't tell Abraham everything that he will be doing in the future- just that he had to leave home and enter the promised land. It takes great faith to trust You with our future, relaxing as the day unravels itself, with all its blessings and challenges. Being present in today is a gift, and we miss this gift when we dwell too much in the past or the future. Being present today allows us to forfeit control of the future, granting us peace in the meantime. Being present today allows us to embrace each and every moment, as if it's our last, giving You glory with everything that we do. Lord, may we be mindful of the past and the future but to spend the most time in the present, so that we don't miss the gift that it is. In Your name we pray. Amen! :)

What is your relationship with your past, present and future like? Are you able to enjoy the present to its fullest, keeping in mind the past and the future without it dictating your present?

241

September 20

Father God, thank You for Your prompting and probing. Our hearts, when left untouched quickly becomes defiled with everything that makes us unclean- but it is with Your Spirit's probing that prompts us to bring our unclean hearts so that You can make them clean again. Our God-given consciences helps to keep us in check, making our hearts uneasy when something is simply not right. Our uneasy hearts cringe when our brothers and sisters are starving and have nothing to eat- prompting us to do something about it. Our uneasy hearts are heavy when our relationship with our neighbor is hurting and filled with resentment, compelling us to make amends and reconcile. Our uneasy hearts burn when we are jealous of our neighbors, revealing our deeper need for Your love more than anything else, prompting us to drop to our knees in Your presence. Lord, may we be receptive when our hearts become uneasy because something is simply not right. In Your name we pray. Amen! :)

How has God's probing in your spirit caused you to draw closer to Him?

September 21

Father God, thank You for wisdom. Wisdom is the practice of right judgement. We are not born with wisdom but slowly accumulate its attributes in our lives. Wisdom is the ability to reconcile with our neighbors quickly before being brought to the judge. Wisdom is taking necessary preliminary steps to avoid sin and stay within the right boundaries. Wisdom is letting go of the futile things of battles in order to win the war. Wisdom is the ability to see danger down the road and decide to change course in order to avoid trouble. Lord, may we recognize wisdom when we see it and embrace it for when we will need to put it to good use. In Your name we pray. Amen! :)

September 22

Father God, thank You for order. Order is the particular arrangement of people and/or things for a particular purpose. We all know You are a God of order and not of chaos with one simple glance at the universe around us. We know that the Church You instituted has an inherent form of order, abiding to the hierarchy that was established. We know that You desire us to lead ordered lives adhering to Your commandments, rather than living in sin and consequently chaos. Lord, may we embrace order in our lives and welcome You into our hearts whenever our hearts may be facing a tumultuous storm. In Your name we pray. Amen! :)

September 23

Father God, thank You for children. Children are the natural course that life takes to perpetuate itself. Aside from being the image of ourselves, children have the capability to demonstrate such powerful spiritual truths. Children are innocent and often see the best in people. Children are carefree, trusting that their parents have everything under control. Children are often regarded as the lowest in the social ladder, but are considered as the greatest in Your eyes. Lord, may we embrace the lessons we learn from the children in our lives, for they truly represent the relationship we should have with You and our neighbors. In Your name we pray. Amen! :)

How have children been a blessing in your life? What truths have you learned from these innocent beings?

September 24

Father God, thank You for mentors. Mentors are role models that we look up to for guidance and direction. Often times, we don't feel like we're ready to be mentors to others when we still have a lot to sort through in our own lives, but there will always be that little someone in our lives that will be walking in our footsteps, whether good or bad. Often times we are so focused on ourselves that we fail to take the time to counsel those around us, missing prime opportunities to share Your perfect love. Often times we don't realize the impact our lives have on other people, thinking that our actions only affect ourselves, but in reality, people are constantly observing and our decisions go far beyond the surface. We are called to be mentors to those around us, especially the little ones You have entrusted to us, effectively passing on the faith, encouraging them when the journey becomes difficult and being the good role models they so desperately need. Lord, help us to embrace opportunities to impart the goodness You have given to us to those around us, especially the children that absorb everything like sponges. In Your name we pray. Amen! :)

What mentors do you have in your life? Who do you find yourself mentoring?

September 25

Father God, thank You for Your providence. As mere humans, we were born into a state of need and continue to believe that we constantly need even when we have been blessed beyond measure. It is up to us to stop our striving and look around at all of our blessings, giving gratitude for all that You have done in our lives. We worry when we don't believe that You have our best interest in mind and would let bad things happen to us. We worry when we feel we don't have control over a situation, even though we never have control of anything in our lives, even our own lives. We worry when we feel that You are holding back from us good things and would rather bless others instead of us. But You are God of the good and the bad, bringing sunshine and rain to them both- we just have to trust You that You are taking care of us, even when we don't feel like You are. Lord, help us to cast all our burdens and worries on You so that our load in life is lighter. In Your precious name we pray. Amen! :)

How has God provided for you in your life? Did He provide in areas that tend to worry you?

September 26

Father God, thank You for new beginnings. Often times we get so caught up in the moment and forget that there will always be a new beginning-we just have to be prepared to receive it. When one door closes, we must actively start to look for the open windows. When we decide to repent and stop sinning, we must look for practical ways to start walking down the path of holiness. When we've been waddling around in darkness for too long, we must decide to strive for the light and be ready for a new way of life. In every life, there are seasons of good and bad, ups and downs, but we must remember that the best is yet to come-we just have to be ready for it-physically, mentally, emotionally and spiritually. Lord, as our lives takes its twists and its turns, may we keep our eyes fixated on You, looking for the new beginnings You bring our way. In Your name we pray. Amen! :)

What new beginnings have come your way? Have you taken advantage of these beginnings to have a fresh start in a new chapter of your life?

Father God, thank You for Your counterintuitive instructions. As mere humans with the tendency towards sin, we ought to act against our flesh and according to Your Spirit. When our first instinct when someone wrongs us is to get revenge, You instruct us to refrain from retaliation, stop the vicious cycle of anger, and trust that You will one day avenge us. When people treat us with hatred and contempt, You desire that we love our enemies and pray for their well-being, giving them grace that they never deserved. When someone steals our tunic, instead of getting it back, You tell us to give them our cloak, creating generous and giving hearts in us, severing our attachment to material goods. For what we don't realize from Your counterintuitive instructions is that, although we seem to be losing when we follow Your directions, we are actually gaining freedom, avoiding the chains of resentment, revenge and hatred that otherwise would bind us and make us prisoners. Lord, may we put into practice the counterintuitive commandments that You have graciously given to us so that we can nurture tender hearts that are free from the chains of sin. In Your awesome name we pray. Amen! :)

What counterintuitive instruction that God has given us have you done recently? How has it liberated you?

Father God, thank You for stillness. In a society where everything is go, go, go- You invite us to stop and relax. Although we have more gadgets to make our lives easier, we find that we continue to fill our lives with things that eat up our time and attention, making us more stressed in the end. Instead of embracing silence and spending some time with You, we plug our ears with headphones to drown out the deafening silence. Instead of taking the long scenic route to just soak in the creation You have blessed us with, we rather jump into our cars and onto the highway to get to our destination quicker. Instead of taking the time to stop and pray, we would rather find another activity to distract us from the emptiness of our lives. Instead of enjoying the journey of life, we try to arrive at our destination as soon as possible, only to find ourselves striving for another destination and goal. Lord, may we understand that sometimes less is more and that stillness is a very beautiful thing we should cultivate. In Your name we pray. Amen! :)

How have you incorporated stillness in your life? How has it enriched it more than filling it with yet another activity to do?

September 29

Father God, thank you for service. Service is when we stop thinking of ourselves and start reaching out to help others. In this society, we are taught to fend for number one, putting us on a pedestal and making us the god of our lives. But we were never meant to sit on a throne like that, but to humble ourselves and take the lowly places. We were never meant to use and abuse others for our benefit, but to help others reach their maximum potential. We were never meant to be totally consumed in ourselves, but to get out of our heads and into the world, making a difference in the best way we know how. Lord, may we lower ourselves and elevate You so that we can better serve the people around us- the way it was always meant to be. In Your name we pray. Amen! :)

How have you served others lately? Has it taken you off the pedestal of your life and given you a better perspective of life?

September 30

Father God, thank You for the simplicity of life. Although we, as mere humans, complicate things beyond comprehension, You show us that the life You desire for us is one of ease and minimal burden. Yes, life gets messy but when we surrender everything to You, there is little left for us to handle. Yes, life can be demanding, but when we prioritize, we realize what's important and what's not. Yes, life gets stressful, but when we realize that we are beyond blessed, we stop thinking of what we don't have and start appreciating all that we do have- cultivating an attitude of gratitude. Lord, may we not make life more complicated than it already is and just soak in Your goodness, giving You praise that You wholeheartedly deserve. In Your name we pray. Amen! :)

How have you complicated life more than it needs to be? How can you uncomplicate it again?

October 1

Father God, thank You for forgiveness. Forgiveness is letting go of someone's debt, whether they deserve it or not. Contrary to the world's standards of obtaining justice and seeking revenge, You tell us to forgive. And better yet, You tell us to forgive indefinitely, even if it's seventy times seven times. You tell us to forgive because You have first forgiven us. You tell us to forgive not for the benefit of our trespasser but for our sake, breaking the chains of unforgiveness and resentment. You tell us to forgive so that we can live together in peace, cultivating an atmosphere of love rather than bitterness and hatred. We may not understand all that You command us to do but we soon realize that You know what's best for us and we should be obedient to Your will. Lord, may we forgive those that have hurt us, even if it's ourselves, in order to fully reap the blessings of Your Spirit. In Your precious name we pray. Amen! :)

What unforgiveness weighs down on your heart today? Do you know the freedom you'll experience if you let it go and move on?

October 2

Father God, thank You for contentment. Being content simply means that we are happy with our blessings and are not looking at other people's blessings, yearning to have that as well. We tend to not realize that everyone has a different story, and that what we can see on the outside is very different from what is happening behind the scenes. We tend to forget that with every blessing, comes with its own set of complications and struggles, which must be taken into consideration. We tend to pinpoint all that other people may have that we don't, but fail to realize that we have our own set of blessings that others may not enjoy. Lord, may we not look around, comparing ourselves to our brothers and sisters, but find complete contentment and satisfaction right where we are. In Your sweet name we pray. Amen! :)

What is your perspective of all that God has blessed you with? Are you satisfied or do you want more? How can you become more content with where you are at now?

October 3

Father God, thank You for the bare necessities. In a society of excess and abundance, we think that getting more is what will fill the void in our hearts. But we don't realize that that void in our hearts is a God-shaped void that only You can fill. We think that since our neighbor has a little more, they must be a little more happy, but fail to realize that joy is rooted in You. We think that accomplishments will make us more important in this world, but fail to realize that our worth is rooted in You, as we are bearers of Your image. We think that having all these fancy gadgets will make our lives easier, but fail to realize that peace ultimately comes from You and cannot be bought. When we realize that everything else in this life is superfluous, we understand that all that we really need is You. Lord, may we not get distracted by all the shiny things of this world, but to solely fix our eyes on You, the true source of peace, joy, love, and life. In Your name we pray. Amen! :)

What are the bare necessities of life? Would you say that you already have them and anything more is just extra?

October 4

Dear God, thank You for the bigger scheme of things. Quite often, we magnify our problems to be bigger than they really are, narrowing down on the details rather than stepping back and seeing how everything unfolds. Quite often, we have our own opinions of how events should have panned out rather than appreciating the beauty behind it all. Quite often, we dwell too much on one particular event that didn't go as planned, and forget to let it go so that we can enjoy everything else. Lord, help us to step back so that we can see Your Hand in all that You're doing in our lives, rather than getting caught up in all the details. In Your precious name we pray. Amen! :)

Do you tend to have the bigger scheme of life in mind or have you fallen into the temptation to magnify the petty little problems? How can you step back and appreciate how the story is unfolding today?

October 5

Father God, thank You for differences. One of humanity's downfalls is the tendency to make others like us. But when we do that, we cut ourselves off from many of Your blessings associated with our differences. It's because of our differences that there is diversity of personalities and abilities, finding their perfect place in our world. It's because of our differences that we can build upon each other's strengths, and support each other in our weaknesses, achieving much more than we ever could alone. It is because of our differences we can better understand and know You, for You are present in each and every one of us as we are bearers of Your image. Lord, may we not see our differences as a point of contention but something that we can embrace and cherish, for it is a blessing in itself. In Your name we pray. Amen! :)

What is your relationship with differences of people in your life? Do you embrace them or avoid them?

"Just as a body, though one, has many parts, but all its many parts form one body, so it is with Christ." – 1 Corinthians 12:12

October 6

Dear God, thank You for delayed gratification. In this microwave generation, everything has to be quick and snappy, grabbing anything in arm's reach to enjoy today. But we all know, in one way or another, that everything worth having takes time and effort. Delaying gratification allows us to intensify the pleasure we would enjoy by abstaining for just a little bit. Delaying gratification allows us to obtain the goals that we desire for the future, simply by setting priorities in its rightful order. Delaying gratification allows us to grow in sanctification by avoiding the alluring temptations of sin, and focusing on the beauty of righteousness. Saying no to certain things today does not necessarily mean forever and always, but simply just not yet. Lord, may we practice the virtue of patience and delay gratification when it's best to, so that we can enjoy an even better version of it in the future. In Your name we pray. Amen! :)

What is your relationship with delayed gratification? Do you tend to delay gratification or do you need to practice it more?

October 7

Father God, thank You for faith. Faith is the belief in something that is not seen. Whether we like to admit it or not, everyone exerts a certain amount of faith every day. We have faith that we will wake up in the morning when we lay our heads to sleep. We have faith that our cars will safely take us from point A to point B, when we hop in to go somewhere. We have faith that our heart will continue to pump, whether or not we are aware of its efforts. Faith is very important for when we lack faith, our lives become chaotic---fearing anything and everything, taking concerns and worries to an unhealthy level. Lord, may we continue to work out our faith that You have everything under control and that we can expect good things to come rather than devastation. In Your name we pray. Amen! :)

How does faith play its role in your life? Do you have faith that everything will be alright or do you tend to worry and try to take things into your own hands? How can you let go and trust more?

October 8

Father God, thank You for those "aha!" moments. "Aha!" moments are moments of epiphany, where everything that has been going around us didn't make sense until one point in time. Those moments are crucial for when we finally see the sin that we live in, and bravely make the decision to repent. Those moments are important for the times that everything that we know about You and Your Son finally makes sense and we decide to enter into a lifelong relationship, changing the course of our lives. Those moments are important for when we finally realize that the goal of life is rather simple: to love You and to love our neighbor- and that we must avoid the many distractions that are thrown our way. Lord, may we embrace these "aha!" moments of clarity, bringing into focus what's really important and what's really true. In Your name we pray. Amen! :)

What "aha" moment have you had recently? How has it drastically changed your life?

October 9

Father God, thank You for setting us free. Freedom from sin is not only relevant to our own personal sins but also the sins of the people around us. Often times people question why bad things happen to good people, but fail to realize that we live in a broken world with sinful people- we may be good people but fall victim to other people's vices. Often times we view freedom as the ability to make our own choices, but fail to realize that true freedom is the ability to live without chains of sin holding us back-either our sin or the consequences of other people's sins. Often times we think that we have to conform to those that are closest to us, even when they live in sin- but fail to realize that we are free to choose our own friends, developing a good support system that nurtures good character. Lord, may we embrace the freedom that You offer us, amidst this broken world, to wholeheartedly follow You. In Your precious name we pray. Amen!

Have you ever wondered why bad things happen to good people? How have you suffered from the consequences of your sins and/or other people's sins?

October 10

Father God, thank You for leaving nothing unnoticed. In a broken world, we are bound to be wronged at least once or twice, if not many times. And naturally we want to retaliate, returning unloving actions for the unloving actions we receive from others. Naturally, we want to look out for number one, pushing all others aside because we've been previously pushed aside. Naturally, we want to forgo all that You have taught us on how to behave towards our neighbor because simply they don't deserve the love that You want us to give. But what we must hold onto and have faith is that nothing goes unnoticed in Your books and all the wrong that have been done to us are accounted for on Judgement day- we just have to be faithful servants doing as we are told until that day arrives or we are called home. Lord, may we understand that all our efforts in being good Christians despite the wrong that we receive is not done in vain but will be rewarded one day. In Your name we pray. Amen! :)

Do you trust that God is watching everything and everything will be accounted for? How does that change your perspective on life? Does it encourage you to continue your faithful walk?

October 11

Father God, thank You for opportunities to overcome selfishness. Selfishness is the tendency to think of ourselves before the needs and desires of others. Although being selfish is a natural innate trait, the nudging of the Holy Spirit leads us to act otherwise. Although selfishness is the result of a belief that we are not worthy, acting against selfishness is believing that we are worthy in God's eyes. Although selfishness is a manifestation of the belief that we don't have enough, acting against selfishness is believing that we are beyond blessed and are ready to bless others. Lord, may we not only overcome the selfishness that we encounter in ourselves but the selfishness that we encounter in others, which may affect us in one way or another. In Your name we pray. Amen! :)

How can you overcome the tendency to be selfish in your daily life? Are you usually successful in being selfless?

October 12

Father God, thank You for surprises. Surprises are things that happen to us without our expectation. Although we tend to like the good surprises, like a little gift waiting for us at home, a surprise birthday party, or a surprise visit by people we love- we tend to get frustrated when it's a surprise that is not very pleasant. Such surprises include situations like our car breaking down and causing us to tap into our savings- making us to humble ourselves and rely on You to get us through the day. Surprises such as bumping into someone that may rub us in the wrong way- making us practice our patience and giving unconditional love. Surprises such as a random change of plans- making us become flexible to accept whatever comes our way. Lord, although we may appreciate stability and constancy, may we learn to embrace all the surprises that we encounter, which ultimately makes life more interesting. In Your we pray. Amen! :)

What surprises have you had in your life recently? Were they good or not-so-pleasant surprises? Did you receive them well?

October 13

Dear God, thank You for eyes to see. Just because we have eyes, does not necessarily mean we can "see" what is really there. Often times, we see all of Your creation- and miss the beauty that was instilled with incredible function. Often times, we take for granted all that has been done for us- and miss all the sacrifice, effort and love that was put into the final product. Often times, we are so caught up with our petty little problems- and fail to see all the blessings that surround us daily. Lord, may we exercise our eyes to really "see" what is out there, focusing on truly how much You love us- despite how we may feel. In Your name we pray. Amen! :)

Do you have the eyes to see what's really there? Has there been any time where you missed something beautiful or profound simply because you didn't *see* it?

October 14

Father God, thank You for all that we can do.
Often times, we compare ourselves to other
people around us or those from the past, and
can't help but feel insignificant and unworthy of
any change- but we forget that the little that
we can do, when given to You, can be multiplied
and create even greater effect than any action
on our own. When we compare ourselves to the
ultimate Saints of the world, we feel as though
we are nearly not as good as they are- but
forget that the saints had struggles of their
own, and yet made such tremendous impact.
When we compare ourselves with those with
influential power, we feel as though we can't
trigger any change- but forget that we
influence people all the time, and one of the
people we do influence may very well become
the president of the United States. When we
compare ourselves with people with money and
fame, we feel as though we just don't have
enough to make a difference- but forget that
the little that we can contribute will take care
of at least one person's need, making the world
with one less problem. Very often, it's not a
question about how much we will help and
contribute, but rather a question of "will we
contribute?". Lord, help us to not focus on all
that we cannot do but rather on all that we
can- making a difference in any way we know
how. In Your name we pray. Amen! :)

October 15

Father God, thank You for perseverance. Perseverance is the ability to push through towards something desired, no matter the obstacles that may come our way. In a "feel-good" society, we are taught to do whatever makes us feel good, regardless if it's actually good- but we forget that it's the good things in life that are often difficult to get. We are taught to quit when the going gets tough, but don't realize that we may just be on the verge of success or passing through the valley to just climb back up on the peak. We are taught to do whatever makes us happy- but forget that true joy comes from You and happiness is fleeting when it is not founded on something good and substantial. Lord, when the going gets tough, grant us the virtue of perseverance to stick it through so that we can attain even greater goodness. In Your name we pray. Amen! :)

What good thing in your life has required a substantial amount of patience and perseverance? Would you say it's worth every ounce of effort on your part?

October 16

Father God, thank You for preparation. Preparation is the act of bringing together and doing what is needed in order to get something properly accomplished. Often times, we want to skip the preparation period and go straight to the finished product- but we fail to realize that the time of preparation is perhaps the most important step of all and either make or break the final product. Often times, we desire to skip the discipline it takes to properly prepare for a major task - but only realize that the successful execution of the major task is only possible with patient preparation. Often times we don't want to sacrifice anything today and want to do it all- but fail to realize that minor sacrifices today, at appropriate times, will yield a better future, one that is worth all the little sacrifices. Lord, may we learn to take seriously times of preparation so that we are better equipped for the future and when certain opportunities present themselves. In Your name we pray. Amen! :)

What is your perspective with times of preparation? Do you welcome it and do your best or do you try to fast forward preparation?

October 17

Father God, thank You for relationships. Relationships are the culmination of all of our interactions with people around us. Sometimes those interactions are positive yielding good vibes and energy and sometimes those interactions are negative, resulting in some conflict- but it's in those negative interactions that we can clearly see our shortcomings. Sometimes relationships act like mirrors, reflecting back to us all of our vices and the ways that we are not perfect- but only so that we can accept our imperfection and work towards perfection. Sometimes we try to surround ourselves with only people who think and act like us- but realize that it's the people who are different that bring new and fresh perspective into our lives, making us grow in ways we never knew were possible. Lord, may we embrace all the different kinds of relationships we encounter throughout our lives, looking to see how we can grow stronger from those relationships. In Your precious name we pray. Amen! :)

How do you tend to approach relationships? Do you try to surround yourself with only people who think and act like you or do you reach out to everyone?

October 18

Father God, thank you for simplicity. Although attaining happiness and peace is rather simple, we tend to complicate things. Instead of trusting You to provide for our needs, we fret and complain about not having "enough"- when in reality we have more than enough. Instead of being grateful for all that we have been blessed with, we dwell and think about all the annoying little details of our lives- and forget all the big positive attributes in our lives. Instead of taking the moment to sit in silence and to be present with You, we like to fill our days to the brim- forgetting that true happiness, peace and joy lies in our relationship with You, our Creator. Lord, may we embrace simplicity in our lives, appreciating the little things in life and cultivating an attitude of gratitude for however much or little we've been blessed with. In Your name we pray. Amen! :)

Do you find yourself complicating your life often? How can we stop and praise God for the life that we already have?

October 19

Father God, thank You for this adventure called life. An adventure is a journey that is unusual, exciting, and typically dangerous at times. Very often, we look to go on an adventure but fail to realize that our lives are adventures themselves. There are never 2 days that are exactly the same, yet our days are numbered so we ought to make the best of each day. There are many obstacles along the way, of which initially we prefer not to encounter them, but when we look back, we can assuredly say they have made our journey a bit more interesting had we not encountered those surprises. There are countless of places to see, people to meet, foods to try, instruments to learn, languages to speak- that we simply don't have the time to be bored and realize that life is simply too short to be anything but happy. Lord, may we embrace this rollercoaster ride of life, making the best out of it as much as we can, dedicating each day to Your greater glory. In Your name we pray. Amen! :)

How has your life been like a rollercoaster? Have you been scared or thrilled throughout your ride? How do you react to twists and turns that inevitably occur in your life?

October 20

Father God, thank You for the ability to stop sin in its tracks. Sometimes we think that since we are wired a certain way, we are destined to commit the same sin over and over again, but that mentality negates our free will and our ability to choose not to sin. Sometimes we continue down a path even though we know it's headed towards sin, but forget that sin is not an overnight process but rather an accumulation of many different decisions that lead towards habitual sin. Sometimes we identify the potential sin that could result and still fall, but forget that You are more concerned about us getting back up again than of our failures. Lord, though we have a tendency towards certain sins, may we identify those sins and do our best to stop them in its tracks before it becomes something even larger- for that is what we are called to do. In Your name we pray. Amen! :)

What sin or vice are you more inclined to do in your life? What can you do to identify it before it happens and stop yourself before you do that particular sin again?

October 21

Father God, thank You for perseverance. Whenever we face opposition, we get tempted to give up, but forget that life is just an accumulation of obstacles and hurdles that we have to get through to reach our goal. Whenever we reach a dead end, we tend to fall into despair, feeling that all of our hard work was for nothing, making us tunnel visioned- but we don't see the numerous alternatives that are available if we would just humbly accept another route. Whenever we hit an all-time low in our lives, we tend to think that You are out to get us and that there is nothing good reserved for us in life- but we forget that after a valley comes the peak of the mountain and we just have to wait to get there. Lord, when times get tough, may we not get discouraged but look for ways that You are working in our lives. In Your name we pray. Amen! :)

How have you persevered in your life? Can you identify when you were at an all-time low and then suddenly, you found yourself at the peak of the mountaintop again?

Father God, thank You for godly advice. As stubborn as we can be, there will come a time in our lives where we have to humble ourselves and seek godly advice. Godly advice come from people who are living righteous lives themselves, yielding tremendous fruit and wish to impart that wisdom upon others. Godly advice is consistent among multiple sources and will not yield conflicting reports because it comes directly from You. Godly advice may not always be what we want to hear, but at the end of the day, points us in the direction that is ultimately best for us. Lord, may we seek and accept godly advice when it is shared with us, even when we don't necessarily agree. In Your name we pray.
Amen! :)

Where do you tend to get godly advice in your life? Do you tend to heed to the advice that you are given?

October 23

Father God, thank You for rest. Rest is the process by which our bodies and souls recuperate after a long journey of work and play. In this busy society, we are tempted to do more work than rest, when in all actuality, resting allows us to do more effective work. We are tempted to play more than we rest, only to find that too much play and little rest can also wear us out and make us miserable. We are tempted to do so much and skip on sleep when in reality, the best life lived is one with a good balance of work, play and rest. Lord, may we embrace appropriate moments of rest so that our bodies and souls can be rejuvenated and reach its maximum potential. In Your precious name we pray. Amen! :)

Do you have a good balance of work, play and rest in your life? How can you improve your balance so that you can live a more fulfilling life?

October 24

Father God, thank You for flexibility. Rather quickly, we come to realize that there is probably more in life that we do not have control over than we do-therefore, developing the skill of flexibility is very important. Flexibility is embracing the change of plans rather than trying everything out of our power to maintain control. Flexibility is appreciating the many different directions life can take and realizing that all will bring You glory. Flexibility is when we relax and see where the ride takes us, having a loose grip on the reigns and trusting that everything will be okay. Lord, may we cultivate the art of being flexible, knowing the delicate balance of sticking to the plan and abandoning the script so that we can appreciate the spontaneity of life all the more. In Your name we pray. Amen! :)

How have you been flexible in your life? Do you feel like you should be more flexible and less controlling? How can you achieve that?

October 25

Father God, thank You for life. Although we quickly find out that life may not be fair, it is still good. Just a quick glance around us is evidence that there is major need in the world-- but that just gives us the opportunity to step up and do something about it. Just a quick glance at our lives and we can easily pin point where we have been wronged and hurt-- but that is an opportunity to grow and forgive, even if the offender is not deserving. Just a quick glance into the future may cause us to become anxious-- but that just gives us the opportunity to trust You no matter what may happen. Lord, may we make the most out of our lives, even if we feel that it's not fair. In Your name we pray. Amen!

October 26

Father God, thank You for self-talk. When the ruler of this world roams around seeking to destroy us, we must be strong and resist temptation. Self-talks help us to speak truth into our lives, ignoring all the lies the enemy feeds us. Self-talk encourages us to keep going even when the enemy wishes we would just give up. Self-talk reminds us of Your promises and keeps them close to our hearts for when we need them most. Lord, may we have good and positive self-talks that help us to be all that You desire us to be. In Your precious name we pray. Amen! :)

October 27

Father God, thank You for oneness. Oneness is characteristic of two distinct entities operating as one unit. As beautiful as it may seem, it is not necessarily easy to act in oneness, for it takes a lot of time, practice and patience. In marriage, 2 people become one and must compromise and learn the other to fully understand how to operate as one. In our relationship with You, we ought to remain in You as You abide in us, and we must remain obedient to Your word in order for that oneness to happen. In the greater world out there, with all of our jobs that require collaboration, we must work together peaceably in order to complete one large unified project. Lord, may we embrace our differences and learn how to work together, operating as one complete entity. In Your name we pray. Amen! :)

What is your experience with the art of becoming one with a unified objective?

Father God, thank You for children. Children is the extension of our lives that propagates Life as a whole. As children are the natural by-product of the love between a man and a woman, they are physical representations of Your love within the Trinity. As children require a lot of time and attention, they force us to be selfless, making us do whatever is best for another and not always for ourselves. As children bring in new energy to a family, the situation of death is manageable as children continue to carry on our legacies in the world. Lord, we thank You for the gift of children and may we be good stewards of the little lives You've entrusted to us. In Your name we pray! Amen! :)

What is your relationship with children? Do you welcome them into your lives and learn from them beautiful realities of life, such as trust and joy? How has children been a blessing in your life?

October 29

Father God, thank You for serenity. Serenity is the state of being calm, peaceful and untroubled. Serenity is not only exclusive for when trouble does not come our way but also during times of utmost disturbance- but we have to be spiritually healthy to believe You have everything under control. Serenity is not only during times when things go our way- but even during times that we have to say "thy will be done" and we don't quite understand why. Serenity is not only reserved for the select few- but is available to everyone and anyone who desires to build and maintain their relationship with You. Lord, may we build our spiritual health in order to cultivate a state a serenity in our lives, during the calm and during the storms. In Your name we pray. Amen! :)

What is your experience with serenity like? Are you able to experience serenity even in the most difficult moments of your life?

October 30

Father God, thank You for deliverance. As we look back on our lives, we can easily see how many times we've been delivered from bad and terrible times- cultivating a spirit of gratitude that we are no longer in those particular situations. Times like those remind us that life is an interesting journey, with its ups and its downs- we just have to go with the flow. Times like those remind us to be thankful when we are not going through the valley or a storm- and to soak in the graces while it lasts. Times like those remind us that a storm will not last forever but will eventually fade away and the sun will start to shine- we just have to be strong enough to wait and withstand the storm while it lasts. Lord, give us the strength to weather the storm, knowing that it will not last forever but it will eventually come to an end and we will be delivered from the valleys of life. In Your name we pray. Amen! :)

Have you been delivered from something terrible in your life? When you look back, do you feel a heavy burden on your heart or do you feel gratitude that you are no longer there?

October 31

Father God, thank You for death. Although society teaches us to avoid death as much as possible, You instruct us to be mindful of death and even to embrace it for it will bring life. Dying to our desires helps us to prioritize what's really important for the sake of the greater scheme of things. The death of our loved ones helps us to remember to continually love one another and express it for we will never know what day will be our last. Death in general reminds us that life is short, our days are numbered and we should make the most out of every day instead of focusing on futile details that bring our spirits down. Lord, may we embrace death as reminders and the means by which life springs forth. In Your precious name we pray. Amen! :)

What is your relationship with death like? Does it bring life or bring you down? How can you grow in situations of death?

November 1

Dear God, in a microwave generation, it is easy to get distracted and waste time. Help us to break away from the fast pace of society and fight for our quiet time with You. It is in this time that we are recharged and regenerated to go back out into the world and love like You have loved us. When everything is competing for our attention, may we be diligent in reserving time for study of Your word and fellowship with You. When there are a million things to do, help us to prioritize our lives so that You are first and everything else comes next. Though there is plenty to do out in the world, may we not forget that internal spiritual growth is most important in order to obtain necessary direction and guidance from the One who knows and sees all. Lord, we know our days are numbered; may we make every moment count with You by our side. In Jesus' name, we pray. Amen! :)

How successful are you in reserving quiet time with God? Do you see a difference in your life when you do compare to when you don't?

November 2

Father God, thank You for internal joy. Internal joy is the joy we experience despite the external circumstances. Very quickly we find that there is quite little that we can control in our lives, and until we surrender the "control" we would like to have, we will be slaves to our own selves. Very quickly, we realize that life can take its sharp twists and turns, drastically changing our whole lives in a matter of minutes, but we must base our happiness not on what's happening around us but on You, the only constant in our lives. Very quickly, we are tempted to believe lies that we are not blessed because so-and-so happened, but need to realize that we live in a broken world and we must make the best out of every circumstance. Lord, may we cultivate a spirit of joy by looking to You for our happiness and not basing it on the circumstances of our lives. In Your mighty name we pray. Amen! :)

Is your happiness dependent on what's happening around you? How can you base your joy on God, who is never-changing?

November 3

Father God, thank You for resistance. Resistance is any force that acts against another source of force. Every day we face some sort of resistance- in good and/or bad ways. Resistance prevents us from spending just that small amount of time with you each day, convincing us that the urgent is more important than everything else- requiring us to actively resist that temptation. Resistance is whatever that gets in between us and the path of righteousness, training us to exercise our spiritual muscles and grow in holiness. Resistance is the stance we take in the face of society, moving against the grain- standing for what is right even if we may be standing alone. Lord, although we tend to desire the easy way out and avoid all forms of resistance, help us to realize that resistance is necessary to maintain healthy bodies and souls. In Your name we pray. Amen! :)

What are the areas of resistance in your life? How have they helped you to grow?

November 4

Father God, thank You for focus. Focus is the ability to shift our attention from everything to anything of importance. In a life full of distractions, we must exercise this muscle of focusing lest we lose sight of our ultimate goal in life. In a life centered around us, we forget that our lives are intended to bring You greater glory through the trials we face. In a life that promises much, we get deceived by the counterfeits surrounding us and forfeit the true joy that is found in You. Lord, help us to maintain focus on You and all that is important so that we can effectively achieve our ultimate goal of sanctification. In Your precious name we pray. Amen! :)

Are you able to focus on what's important and ignore all the distractions surrounding us on a daily basis? How has that ability helped you towards your goals in life?

Father God, thank You for the old and the new. Often times we are so enticed with what's new and flashy but forget the gems of old; however, we ought to embrace both the old and the new. While we make new friends all the time, we should not neglect our old friends for they have a refined friendship that can only come with time. While we tend to only look forward to the future, we must not forget our past for that is where we come from and have learned many lessons of life up till now. While the young are full of life and spirit, we must not neglect our elderly, for they have done their due diligence in taking care of us and are reservoirs of history, experience and advice that they wish to impart. While we tend to focus on the New Testament of the Bible, we must not forget our roots in the Old Testament, for it helps shape the story of the new for our greater understanding. Lord, help us to embrace both the old and the new, for they are equally important in our lives. In Your name we pray. Amen! :)

What old areas of your life must you embrace more? How can that enhance your life and make you a better person?

November 6

Father God, thank You for baby steps. Baby steps are simply small steps that we take towards a larger goal. It's the baby steps that takes something so insurmountable and makes it seem small and achievable, if only we continually work at it. It's the baby steps that allow us to get out of the dark and into the light by breaking addictions, reversing our vices and resisting temptations. It is the baby steps that allows us to achieve such tremendous goals in life, pushing our limits to the skies, accomplishing our dreams, and strengthening our virtues. Lord, may we not be daunted by the massiveness of some of the projects we desire to achieve in life, but be encouraged by the feasibility of the baby steps we can take. In Your precious name we pray. Amen! :)

What baby steps have you taken recently in your life? What baby steps *should* you be taking, if you haven't been already?

November 7

Father God, thank You for the ability to listen. Listening is an art of physically hearing the words of another and mentally processing it to make sense of the words. Often times, we are so distracted and only "half listen" and just hear our neighbors but don't necessarily listen to them, making the process of communication incomplete and ineffective. Often times, we try to multitask and think or do other things while we are "listening" to our neighbors, but realize that with divided attention, we are doing neither task to the best of our abilities and are just wasting our time. Often times, we successfully hear and process what our neighbor is trying to express to us, but it takes a compassionate heart to actually consider what is being said and do something about it. Lord, may we embrace the lost art of listening to hear our neighbor's concerns in order to live in greater harmony with each other. In Your precious name we pray. Amen! :)

Do you truly exercise the beautiful art of listening? Are you able to see behind what's really being said with undivided attention? How has listening impacted your life or someone you know?

November 8

Father God, thank You for the ability to praise. Praise is the expression of approval and admiration towards another being. Though we were created to praise, we find ourselves praising the wrong things like celebrities, cars, sports teams, clothes, fame, money, etc. when we really should be praising You. Though we may not like everything that has happened in our lives, praising You through it all allows our hearts to remain in a state of gratitude. Though there may be less than 100 things to be sad about, there are thousands of things to be happy about, and praising Your name allows us to realize that we are blessed on a daily basis. Lord, may we embrace the art of praising Your name from the moment we rise up from bed to the setting of the sun each and every day. In Your mighty name we pray. Amen! :)

Do you cultivate an attitude of praises? Do you find yourself praising God even through the storms? How can you exercise the practice of praising in your life?

Father God, thank You for the Trinity. The Trinity is the description of You being 3 separate entities yet still one God. Although this concept seems too difficult for us to wrap our minds around as mere humans with limited understanding, You give us numerous examples in daily life that help us to understand. As the Holy Spirit is the direct expression of love emanating between You, the Father and Your Son, a child is the direct representation of the love between a man and a woman creating one family unit. As water can exist as liquid, ice or gas- it's still water at the end of the day with the molecular formula of H_2O with 3 different forms. As the sun can demonstrate its presence in multiple ways- 1) as the sun itself, a massive star continually burning gases of helium and hydrogen, 2) as the light that is emitted continuously bringing life to everything on earth, and 3) as the warm rays that is emanated from the sun and light, bringing comfort to an otherwise cold world. Lord, may we embrace all of Your entities in order to fully know who You are. In Your precious name we pray. Amen! :)

Do you have a relationship with all 3 aspects of the Holy Trinity? How does your relationship with each differ from the other?

November 10

Father God, thank You for seasons. Seasons are the times in our lives that are significantly different from another times due to various factors. Seasons come and go, helping us to realize that the season we are currently in is not going to last forever and will eventually change for the good or the bad. Seasons remind us that there are appropriate times to be happy and appropriate times to be sad- as there is a time for everything and each emotion is good in its proper time. Seasons help us to differentiate one season from another, allowing us to appreciate the uniqueness of each season- including the changes in scenery when we move, the different people around us, different positions we attain, and significant changes in our relationships. Lord, may we embrace each season for what it's worth, making the best out of it for Your greater glory. In Your mighty name we pray. Amen! :)

Do you recognize the different seasons in your life as they come and go? What is your relationship with seasons?

Dear God, thank You for pouring truth into our hearts. As it is important to not believe lies, it is also important to fill our minds with truth. Although we think that words are weak and don't have much influence, what we say to others and to ourselves can impact us in ways we never knew possible- which is why we must forgo the lies and embrace the truth. Although we may not be who we want to be or where we want to be in life at the moment, we must declare those desires now so that our dreams will one day become a reality. Although we tend to look out and fend for ourselves, we must also speak life into others for as they rise up to their greatest potential, you rise up with them- as we are all one team. Lord, may we speak truth into our lives and believe it until they become reality, for words are stronger than we may think. In Your precious name we pray. Amen! :)

What lies must you relinquish and what truth must you start embracing? Do you help others to rise above the lies and take in the truth?

November 12

Father God, thank You for Your relentless love for us. Your unrelenting love for us has sought us out in our sin, and still loved us unconditionally- the way we should love our spouse in marriage. Your unrelenting love provides us with hope of a better future, one in which we are reunited back with You- which reflects the hope of a lost child or loved one, one day coming back home to the family. Your unrelenting love gives us the motivation to exhibit unrelenting love in our own relationships, whether or not the person we are loving is reciprocating that love back to us. Lord, may we accept Your relentless love as an example of how we should love others for Your greater glory. In Your precious name we pray. Amen! :)

How is God's unrelenting love towards us helping you to show that same love towards others in your life? Is it as easy as it seems?

November 13

Dear God, thank You for respect. Respect is the attitude we harbor to show honor to another person or thing. Although respect is being lost in our society today, we must work against this common culture and instill it back into the threads of our humanity. Respect in a marriage allows for love to flourish, creating a beautiful cycle of love and respect between a man and a woman. Respect for human life allows for others with a strong position to help and defend the lives of those without a voice, namely the unborn children falling victims to abortion. Respect of the Holy allows us to respect You, our God and know our position as mere humans. Lord, help us to cultivate a demeanor of respect in all that we do. In Your mighty name we pray. Amen! :)

How has our society lost the important act of respect? How can we bring it back?

November 14

Father God, thank You for teaching us. With just a quick glance over our lives, we can pinpoint all the times that You have done something in our lives to teach us an important truth, for the ultimate purpose of our sanctification. You teach us in many ways, including disciplining us to prevent us from going down one path and leading us to another, for You know what lies ahead and are guiding us to do Your will. You teach us by not giving us everything we want at the time we want it so that we can learn the beauty of delayed gratification and being patient for the blessing You have in store for us. You teach us through others speaking hard truths to us in order to change our hearts and prepare ourselves for greater blessings up ahead. Lord, when things don't go our way, instead of kicking and pouting, may we step back and ask for what it is that You may be trying to teach us. In Your name we pray. Amen! :)

What and how has God taught you in your life? Did you receive the lessons with an open heart or did you put up a fight?

November 15

Father God, thank You for the silver lining. In every situation, we can focus on the heavy clouds looming directly over us or we can look for the silver lining that makes the heavy rain clouds tolerable and even beautiful. In every situation, the ones that go according to our plans and the ones that don't, we can try to see the blessings instead of what went "wrong" or what could go wrong. In every situation we encounter in life, we have the decision to wait for the storm to pass or learn how to dance in the rain. Lord, may we learn to look for the silver lining in every circumstance in our lives so that we can give You glory in everything. In Your precious name we pray. Amen! :)

November 16

Dear God, thank You for action. Action is the process of doing something. You are not so concerned as to what we say but the obedience that follows what we say, which reflects the love that we have for You. When talk is cheap and words are plentiful, it's the sacrifice behind our actions that fully demonstrate the love and intention that we wish to portray. Although the words we say sound lovely and express our willingness to do something, it's the actual action that makes all the difference. Lord, may we not only have the willingness to follow Your word but also the ability to do it, for it's our actions that matter anyways. In Your precious name we pray. Amen! :)

November 17

Dear God, thank You for seeds. Seeds are little intricate structures containing the complex biological information to recreate yet another plant much bigger than the seed and has the potential to create more seeds. Such a concept is fundamental in our walk as everything that we do in faith are little seeds that we spread out to cultivate into something beautiful. Such a concept encourages us to be generous with our time, talent and treasure for we do not know how far You can make it grow in Your kingdom. Such a concept helps us to be generous with our encouragement towards others on this rather discouraging walk of life, for we would never know the impact a few kind words, a smile and/or a hug could have on someone's life. Lord, help us to be little seeds in all that we do during our short time on earth, trusting that our little actions will take root and become something even greater than ourselves. In Your name we pray. Amen! :)

What seeds have you been planting recently? Do you acknowledge that God can take your small seeds that you planted and make it grow into something bigger than you can imagine?

"Still other seed fell on good soil, where it produced a crop—a hundred, sixty or thirty times what was sown." – Matthew 13:8

297

November 18

Father God, thank You for the "weeds" in our lives. Weeds are the children of the enemy growing together with the wheat. Although we would much rather have the weeds already removed from our lives so that our lives are much easier otherwise, we forget that You desire salvation for everyone and that none may perish. Although some weeds may look beautiful and may be disguised as flowers, we must have a discerning heart to stay away from deceitful weeds. Although the weeds in our lives make our lives considerably more difficult, they also help sanctify us as we are put through different trials testing our character and faith. Lord, where there are weeds, may they be opportunities for us to pray, discern and be sanctified, for Your greater glory. Amen! :)

Who are the weeds in your life? Do you continue to show them love and respect, praying that one day they will change from their ways? How are you sanctified through the weeds in your life?

"'No,' he answered, 'because while you are pulling the weeds, you may uproot the wheat with them." – Matthew 13:29

November 19

Father God, thank You for divine revelation. Divine revelations are messages coming directly from You with a specific divine purpose of ultimately bringing You glory. Many times, we encounter stirrings of the Holy Spirit, pulling on our heart strings to make necessary changes to our lives- and we would be wise to listen and act upon those nudges. Many times, we have a supernatural experience that cannot be explained by natural means but are just little reminders that there is a supernatural component to our existence. Many times, events in our lives are orchestrated in such a way that clearly shows divine intervention and we should not fight the guidance of Your Spirit but be fine-tuned to the direction that You are leading us. Lord, may we be mindful of these divine revelations so that we can grow closer to You in our relationship and walk down the path You wish for us to walk. In Your name we pray. Amen! :)

What divine revelations have you experienced in your life? How have they impacted you?

November 20

Father God, thank You for grace. Grace is the good things we receive even when we don't deserve it. Through the grace that we receive from You, we can learn to expend the same grace towards others, even when it's not easy. Through the grace that we extend to others, we still hold them to high expectations and standards, but can still bless them even when they fall short. Through the grace that we expend on each other, we allow room for growth, in ourselves and in others. Lord, may we show grace to our neighbors, especially the ones that repeatedly fail us, for they are the ones that tend to hurt the most and matter the most. In Your name we pray. Amen! :)

November 21

Father God, thank You for mentors. Mentors are people in our lives that can help guide us through life and navigate through the complex situations we encounter. The elders in the church serve as mentors as they pass down accurate theology, relevant traditions and proper way of worship. The elders in our lives have experience in life and can dispense valuable wisdom to us that we otherwise wouldn't have access to. The elders closest to us can know all the dirty details of our lives and can share important advice that may help us avoid devastation later down the road. Lord, may we identify the elders You have placed in our lives that can help us effectively navigate through life. In Your mighty name we pray. Amen! :)

Father God, thank You for reminders. Reminders are simply normal and ordinary things that are set aside with the specific intention of reminding us of something important. You know very well that the human heart is forgetful and have commanded Your people on numerous occasions to build a monument to remind them of some miraculous deed You performed for them. Our founding fathers found it necessary to set aside specific days to celebrate important aspects of our history as reminders of how far we've come. Our first president saw the importance of being thankful to You, our Lord for all Your wonderful blessings, and decided to make Thanksgiving an official national holiday with the first Proclamation of Thanksgiving back in 1789. In a world full of distraction, may we continue to practice this art of reminding whatever is deemed worthy of reminding. Lord, help us to remember and keep in mind all of Your promises and may we keep abreast all that is wonderful and worthy of praise. In Your name we pray. Amen! :)

Father God, thank You for editing. Editing is the practice of removing the bad and polishing for a good final product. Believe it or not, we do a lot of editing in our memories, focusing on the good memories that bring us joy and being mindful of the not-so-good memories to learn and mature in our walk. Believe it or not, we do a lot of editing in our relationships as we don't keep track of the wrongs our loved one makes but start off a new day with a clean slate. Believe it or not, we do a lot of editing when we have patience and overlook a lot of the irritable things people do so that we can maintain peace throughout the day. Lord, may we learn to "edit" our lives properly so that we focus on the good, give grace and pray for a better future.
In Your name we pray. Amen! :)

What editing have you done in your life?
What editing should you start doing?

November 24

Father God, thank You for breaks. Breaks are simply time away from something, some place or someone. In a world of non-stop chaos and commotion, we need a break from everything in order to rejuvenate and keep going. Breaks from places such as work and school allows us to come back refreshed with a new spirit ready to tackle on anything. Breaks from things like cell phones, TV, cars etc. help us appreciate the luxuries we have been blessed with and develop the right relationship with these objects. Breaks from people we encounter daily help us to appreciate our loved ones for who they are and spark up the relationship again, giving it new air and perspective. Lord, may we take the appropriate breaks throughout our lives in order to freshen up our spirit and keep going with renewed vigor. In Your name we pray. Amen! :)

How has breaks from your daily life changed your perspective of your life? Do you take breaks frequently?

November 25

Father God, thank You for boundaries.
Boundaries are certain limitations as to where
we and others are not permitted to cross, for
our best interest or the best interest of others.
Boundaries are healthy conditions that help
maintain good relationships between people, as
they do not let one party to step over another,
when the boundaries are truly respected.
Boundaries help to maintain justice as it clearly
defines one's wrongdoing if the boundaries have
been crossed, and certain actions must be taken
in order to rectify the situation. Boundaries
keep us safe and on the right track to live the
best possible life one could live, away from
grave sin and down the paths of righteousness.
Lord, may we embrace and respect the
boundaries placed in our lives so that we can
live as good and holy citizens in Your kingdom.
Amen! :)

Do you set a lot of healthy boundaries in
your life? Do you enforce them? How have
they been beneficial in maintaining order?

November 26

Father God, thank You for continuous improvement. Continuous improvement is the practice of taking baby steps towards a greater and better goal. When we become complacent in our lives is when we stop growing and become stagnant- but we're not called to be stagnant like the Dead Sea but rather vibrant like the Jordan River. When we become complacent in our lives, we harbor pride with the notion that there is no room for improvement and become resistant to any inclination towards greatness. When we become complacent in our lives, we miss out on all the blessings You have in store for us, if only we would humble ourselves and allow us to be molded into Your image. Lord, may we not grow complacent in our lives but continuously look for ways we can grow in body, mind and soul. In Your precious name we pray. Amen! :)

In what areas of your life would you say you've grown complacent? How can you stir it up and continue to grow in that particular area?

November 27

Father God, thank You for ignorance. Ignorance is the lack of knowledge related to something. Although ignorance tends to be seen in a negative light, ignorance at times is better than knowing. Ignorance of how much our peers are getting paid prevents us from comparing our wages, which then tends to make us feel miserable. Ignorance of what's happening in other people's lives helps us to live our lives more genuinely and authentically, instead of continuously comparing our lives to others. Ignorance of what other people think of us helps us to live true to ourselves and be the person we were created to be, without the influence of other people's opinions. Ignorance of all the things that could possibly go wrong helps us to be fearless and brave, trusting that all will fall into place. Lord, may we embrace ignorance wherever it helps us to grow and be the best-version-of-ourselves. In Your name we pray. Amen! :)

How has ignorance been bliss in your life? Is it necessary for us to know all the details in life or is it best sometimes to be ignorant and live genuinely?

Father God, thank You for closed doors. Closed doors are the avenues to certain pathways that are no longer available to us. Although we tend to get discouraged when we encounter a closed door, they help us look for the open window on the other side. Although closed doors may make us feel unloved by You, the One who can open doors, but it forces us to trust You, knowing that You are all we need and not the open doors. Although closed doors may make us feel insecure about ourselves, they are opportunities to grow in humility, accept life as it is and move forward. Lord, thank You for the closed doors in our lives, leading us towards the life You have for us and building the character You wish for us to develop. In Your name we pray. Amen! :)

What closed doors have you encountered in your life? How did they make you feel? Did it force you to look for the open window on the other side?

November 29

Father God, thank You for the benefit of the doubt. The benefit of the doubt is believing the good whether or not we are certain of it. Although it's difficult, we ought to give the benefit of the doubt on a constant basis if we ever hope to build strong and lasting relationships. When we doubt that You will intervene and bless us, its best that we believe You will so that hope will thrive in our hearts. When we doubt that our neighbor will keep their promises, it's best that we trust that they will, while still maintaining healthy boundaries in case that they don't. When we doubt our significance and worth, it's best that we believe we are invaluable and irreplaceable, to give us the drive to keep pushing forward and excel in life. When we doubt the love of a loved one, may we believe that they do regardless of certain actions that may convince us otherwise. Lord, may we continue to give the benefit of the doubt, to others, to You and to ourselves- for it allows for greater growth. In Your name we pray. Amen! :)

Do you tend to give the benefit of the doubt? How can you start doing that more often? How can it help improve the quality of the relationships in your life?

November 30

Father God, thank You for devastations in our lives. Devastating events are life changing times that put us through a series of tests and trials, only to make us stronger in the end. It is not long before we realize that there will be many natural disasters that will essentially take everything we have away in a matter of hours, but these times give us opportunities to rise up and gather together to help our neighbors. It is not long for us to realize that we may face devastation in our own personal affairs, instantly changing the course of our lives in a matter of minutes, but we must look for the silver lining and see how this is actually an act of grace, leading us to a better future than we could ever have imagined. It is not long to see how life can truly be unfair, but the devastations that happen around us teach us to not be a "victim" but a victor, winning the many battles that may come our way. Lord, may we come together during times of devastation and take each day, one day at a time until we can say we have overcome the unexpected. In Your name we pray! Amen! :)

What devastations in your life have you experienced? How have you overcome these devastations? Did it make you stronger in the end?

December 1

Dear God, thank You for support. Support is the aide we receive from others when times get tough. In a world of uncertainty, we need the wisdom of our elders to help us pave down the path we should take in life, based on their past experiences. In a world of evil, we need to see the good in our loved ones and others around us to give us the fuel to keep fighting and believe in a better world. In a world of chaos, we need our righteous neighbors to show us that order and productivity are possible in the midst of a mess. In a world of brokenness, we need our family and friends to help us grow and get back on our feet when it's just too hard to stand on our own. Lord, may we develop a good support system in our lives so that when disaster strikes, we will be able to resist, survive and thrive. In Your name we pray. Amen! :)

Why is a good support system essential to succeed in life? Do you have a good support system? How can you build a better one?

December 2

Father God, thank You for flexibility. Flexibility is being able to bend in the midst of a strong and unrelenting force. It doesn't take much time for us to realize that we need to be flexible in many areas of our lives, in order to be good and functional people. We need to be flexible with our plans, for our lives may never go according to our plans, but we must make the best of it. We must be flexible with people, for they will fail us countless times, but we are still called to love them unconditionally. We must be flexible with ourselves, for we often fail to be the person we want to be, but we must keep picking ourselves up and strive for that ideal. Lord, may we exercise flexibility in all areas of our lives, so that we can bend when needed and come back when the force is withheld. In Your mighty name we pray. Amen! :)

How have you been flexible in your life? Are you able to bend just enough according to the circumstances? Why is being flexible important to ensure we don't break?

December 3

Dear God, thank You for habits. Habits- good and bad- are practices in life that we do often. As creatures of habit, it's important for us to develop good habits to live a good and fulfilling life. Good habits help us to resist temptation with greater ease than someone who has not developed the skill. Good habits help us build better character as character is developed over time through the tests and trials we face in life. Good habits help us break through the resistance that prevents us from doing good practices, allowing us to develop even better habits throughout our lives. Lord, may we realize that habits do not develop overnight but require lots of dedication, which will pay off in the end. In Your name we pray. Amen! :)

What good habits have you developed in your life? What bad habits do you do that you should probably change? What are you doing to change them?

December 4

Father God, thank You for selflessness. Selflessness is when we don't think about ourselves but think about others and everyone's greater good. As selfish people, the virtue of selflessness does not come naturally, but requires tremendous aide from the Holy Spirit to give us strength. As selfish people, we are taught to look out for ourselves and to push aside anyone who may be causing unhappiness- but we are called to greatness, and greatness often times comes with great suffering. As selfish people, we tend to see what benefits us as an individual but fail to strive towards what benefits everyone as a whole, which far outweighs any individual benefit. As selfish people we want instant gratification in the here and now, but fail to sacrifice for an even greater reward in the future. Lord, may we learn to become more selfless in our approach in life, for Your greater glory. In Your name we pray. Amen! :)

Why is being selfless important for you and for everyone around you? How can we become more selfless and think of ourselves less?

December 5

Dear God, thank You for community. Community is a unified body of individuals with a common interest that can be found in nearly every aspect of our lives. The faith community we find at church helps us to stay focused and maintain our relationship with You, our God. The community we find with our colleagues at school or work enable us to help each other as we strive for greater and bigger aspirations. The community we find with our friends allows us to celebrate the good times and support each other during the difficult times with no passing judgement. The community we find with our families at home allows us to be completely ourselves, with all guards down, so that we can see the rawest form of our being, truly exposing all that needs to be sanctified. Lord, may we embrace all the communities in our lives, enriching our lives to its maximum potential. In Your precious name we pray. Amen! :)

Do you tend to participate in the different communities in your life or do you tend to isolate yourself? How do the communities in your life help sanctify you?

December 6

Father God, thank You for puzzle pieces. Puzzle pieces are individual components that may not make sense alone but create a bigger picture when connected to other entities. It doesn't take long for us to realize that life is pretty much a large puzzle that we have to learn how to piece together. Puzzles teach us that we must be patient in order to slowly but surely connect each piece together to make one larger picture. Puzzles teach us that it is important to work off of a master picture on the back of the box, serving as a road map in order to see the bigger picture even before it materializes. Puzzles teach us that certain pieces must be in place in order for other pieces to be attached, showing us that we should do things in a certain order before everything starts to make sense. Lord may we see life as one big puzzle with the many pieces that will fall into place when we develop techniques that help us to piece everything together. In Your name we pray. Amen! :)

How is your life a big puzzle? Do you often find yourself puzzled about the different pieces in your life only to realize that they make sense in conjunction with other pieces? What can puzzles teach you about life?

December 7

Dear God, we thank You for rules and regulations. Although we feel that rules were made to be broken, they are necessary in order to prevent chaos and create progress. Rules and regulations provide us with boundaries that keep us safe so that we all can live and play nicely together. Rules and regulations may not make sense to us but it was established for a reason and should be respected, within certain limits that abide by Your Greater Law. Rules and regulations help us to humble ourselves and realize our place in society, respecting people with authority, whom are entrusted with the responsibility to enforce certain statutes. Lord, may we obey the rules and regulations in our lives, ultimately honoring You with our actions.
In Your name we pray. Amen! :)

What is your relationship with rules and regulations?

December 8

Father God, thank You for tolerance. While tolerance has many meanings, one definition is the capacity to endure much pain and hardship. With the recent horrendous shooting just in our backyard, there is not much good we can see in such an event other than people coming together in the face of tragedy. With the largest shooting ever committed in US history, we can see how much evil is in the world and how much we need You, our God, in our lives. With 50 lives lost, 400 wounded and the shooter committing suicide, we are all called to prayer, not only for the victims but also the shooter and his family- for they are also in pain and are in need of Your saving grace. Lord, may we grow stronger as a nation in the face of this terrible event, inflicting such terrible and horrendous pain in our hearts. In Your name we pray. Amen!

:)

What tragedy has happened in society recently? How can that be used for God's greater glory?

December 9

Father God, thank You for opportunities. Opportunities are simply chances that we are given for advancement or progress in any department of life. While we don't often look for opportunities but somehow stumble across them, we ought to be prepared when we encounter these given opportunities. We need to prepare our minds to accept opportunities when they come our way, and not let them pass thinking we would not be good candidates. We need to prepare our hands to have the skill-set necessary to excel at that opportunity, which is an ongoing process and doesn't stop at any given time. We need to prepare our hearts to have the desire to meet a need, whether it be at church, school, with loved ones or complete strangers, when an opportunity of need arises in our path. Lord, may our eyes be open to the many opportunities that come our way, big ones and small- and may we be prepared to accept that opportunity. In Your name we pray, amen!

:)

Why is it important to prepare your mind, heart and hands to properly receive the opportunities that are given to us? What do you do to prepare for opportunities that come your way?

December 10

Dear God, thank You for today. While yesterday is history and tomorrow is a mystery, today is a gift we must embrace. Although every point of time is important, including the past and future, it's important to have the correct view of each: the past in the rear view, the future with a clear view and being fully present with the best view of today. Although we ought to prepare for our future and learn from our past, but we must not live in our future or our past but rather in our present- lest we become consumed by our future and past and forget to live in the present. Although we are tempted to put off for tomorrow what we could do today, we are not guaranteed tomorrow so let us embrace the blessings and opportunities of today. Lord, may we have the proper relationship of our past, present and future, spending the most valuable time mentally in the present. In Your precious name we pray. Amen! :)

Why is it important to live in the present? Do you find yourself living in the past or the future more than you are in the present? How can you change that?

December 11

Father God, thank You for hospitality. Hospitality is the art of using the gifts we have been blessed with and sharing it with others. Being hospitable towards others expresses a sense of gratitude of the gifts that we have been entrusted with and desire to share them with our neighbors for their enjoyment as well. Being hospitable expresses that everyone is a gift in themselves, and extending friendly treatment means that we are grateful for their presence in our lives. Being hospitable allows us to open up our homes and lives to others so that we are more blessed than we started out, with laughter and good vibes filling the walls and our hearts. Lord, may we grasp every opportunity to be hospitable towards others, strangers and guests alike, for when we are hospitable to the least among us, we are hospitable to You. In Your name we pray. Amen! :)

Are you hospitable towards others? Do you enjoy sharing the blessings you have for the enjoyment of others and yourself? Why is it good to be hospitable?

"Do not forget to show hospitality to strangers, for by so doing some people have shown hospitality to angels without knowing it." – Hebrews 13:2

December 12

Dear Father, thank you for pain. Pain is the unpleasant feeling we experience when something is not ideal. Although we try to avoid pain as much as possible, pain is what makes us human and should be expected in our lives. Pain in our physical bodies allows us to appreciate the times we don't have pain all the more. Painful moments such as the impending death of a loved one helps us to appreciate every precious moment we have left with them on this earth. Pain in our lives allows us to have compassion on others who may be in pain, for we know just how difficult it may be and should do all that we can do to help alleviate their pain. Lord, may we acknowledge the pain we feel in this life and use it to bring about good. In Your name we pray. Amen :)

What is your relationship with pain? Do you find yourself trying to avoid it as much as possible? How can pain be used for good?

December 13

Dear God, thank You for community. Community is the people around us that we do life with. As social beings, we cannot live isolated and must interact with others, lest we go insane and collapse under the pressures of this world. Community consists of the people we see day to day, comprising of our co-workers, authority figures and the people that allow us to make a living- they are there to carry our load when we simply cannot carry it on our own. Community consists of the people closest to our hearts-our immediate family, closest friends and other loved ones- that are the stakes we lean on when our foundation gets weak and tested, helping us to keep standing. Community consists of extended family and friends, of whom we don't see quite often but still mean a lot to us and come together to celebrate and witness life's greatest milestones, including births, baptisms, weddings, and deaths. Lord, may we embrace the community You have blessed us with, both immediate and extended community that come together to live life together. In Your precious name we pray. Amen!

What makes up the community in your life? How do they enhance your life?

December 14

Father God, thank You for serenity. Serenity is the state of being calm, peaceful and untroubled. In a world with so much going on, our peace can easily be robbed- but when we fixate our eyes on You, no storm can steal our joy. In a world where we feel so small and mundane, keeping You in focus helps keep us energized and know our significance. In a world of so much uncertainty, trusting in You helps us believe that nothing can go wrong with You in control. Lord, no matter the day or the season, may we always keep You in focus, the source of our joy and peace. In Your name we pray. Amen!

:)

How can you stay serene and peaceful in your life? Is your joy dependent on your external circumstances or God, who is never-changing?

December 15

Father God, thank You for being sufficient. It doesn't take long for us to realize that our hearts are restless, desperately seeking all that may satisfy the big void in our hearts. Although we may receive love from others, the only satisfying love is from You, which compensates for any love that we may lack. Although we may find significance in what we do, what we wear and what people think of us, the only complete approval is from You, granting us significance for just who we are and not dependent on what we do. Although we may find happiness in external circumstances and the places we visit, but the ultimate source of joy is rooted in You, which is not dependent on anything that may change. Lord, thank You for allowing us to find supplemental sources of love, significance and happiness, but finding the complete and unfailing source in You. In Your name we pray. Amen! :)

Is God all-sufficient for you or do you find yourself trying to fill in the void with people, places and things? How can we be fully satisfied with the love, peace and joy that comes from God?

December 16

Father God, thank You for awareness.
Awareness is the state of knowing what is going
on around us and within us. Awareness is
important for without something being brought
to our attention, it will never be addressed.
Awareness is important because if what we are
doing is sinful and we don't know, either if it's a
sin or if we are even doing it, we will never
come to repentance and change our ways.
Awareness is important for our neighbor may be
sinning or in need, and if we are not attentive,
we may never see the opportunity to do what
we can do to remedy the situation. Lord, may
we be aware, both inner and outer environments,
so that we can bring greater glory to Your
name. In Your precious name we pray. Amen! :)

Has there ever been a time that you were
sinning and didn't know it? How can awareness
help us address what needs to be addressed?

December 17

Father God, thank You for generosity. Generosity is being freely giving with what we have already been blessed with. Giving is not only good for others as we meet their desires and needs but it is also good for our souls, as we continually purge of our attachment to material possessions. Giving is an expression of gratitude, for we give because we are already satisfied with what we have and may have extra to share with our neighbor- for we are only rich if we can share. Giving is an expression of humility, stooping low to serve others with our time, talent and treasure, regardless if they can pay back, but in hopes of them paying it forward. Lord, may we practice the virtue of giving, for it is nourishing for our souls and creates a pleasant atmosphere amongst our neighbors. In Your sacrificial name we pray. Amen! :)

How is giving good for our spiritual growth? What is your attitude about giving? Do you give freely or do you tend to hold onto what is not really yours and only lent to you?

December 18

Father God, thank You for gratitude. Gratitude is the attitude of appreciation which opens up the doors to many more opportunities of growth. Having the eyes of gratitude allows us to be thankful for even things we take for granted each and every day, such as our very lives, the ability to walk, see, feel, taste, hear and smell. Having the eyes of gratitude sees even the slightest improvement or change of anything, giving us the energy and motivation to keep pushing towards our ultimate goal. Having the eyes of gratitude changes our overall demeanor, creating a pleasant atmosphere of positive vibes, which makes room for more positive energy.

Lord, help us to embrace the attitude of gratitude for even the smallest of things in our lives, for it will make a world of a difference. In Your name we pray, amen! :)

December 19

Father God, thank You for time off. Time off is the time we can take to be away from our daily routines. During this time off, we can rejuvenate our spirits, bringing in new air and energy. During this time off, we can heal from the beating of overwhelming situations that we may face on a normal basis. During this time off, we can sit down and re-prioritize what's important in our lives, taking a step back from all the commotion of daily living. Lord, in the hectic lives that we live, may we learn how to take time off to refuel and rejuvenate, so that we can continue to give you our best. In Your name we pray. Amen! :)

December 20

Dear God, thank You for pressure. Pressure is any force exerted in a direction of resistance in our lives. It doesn't take long for us to realize that life is full of pressure from all directions and we can either succumb to pressure or get strengthened from pressure. We experience pressure in our careers, pushing us to limits we never thought were possible- but we must be careful to have a good work/life balance. We experience pressure in our finances and daily living, which allows us to live a certain standard of life, but we must be wise with our resources and live within our means. We experience pressure from loved ones and in our relationships, allowing us to learn and grow from each other, but we must also learn to create healthy boundaries. Lord, may we identify certain sources of pressure in our lives and choose to grow into stronger and more well-rounded individuals. In Your name we pray. Amen! :)

How is pressure used to help you grow, physically, emotionally and spiritually?

December 21

Father God, thank You for charity. Charity is when the needs of our neighbor are being met by another. It doesn't take long for us to realize that resources are not evenly distributed amongst people around the world and there are many that are left starving while there are few that have an overabundance. Although the hunger problem around the world can be easily resolved by a simple snap of Your fingers, You desire to create a giving heart in those that have to give to those that don't have. Although the war-stricken turmoil refugees face on a daily basis can be easily obliterated by a simple command from Your lips, You wish for us to open up our hearts and take care of those that have been displaced from their homes and families. Although the emotional distress people face on a daily basis can be eliminated by a simple breath from Your Holy Spirit, You desire for us to reach out to our neighbors and help provide healing through prayer and the kind words of encouragement we speak to each other. Lord, may we embrace every opportunity to take care of our neighbors in any need that they may have, for we are truly taking care of You at the end of the day. In Your name we pray. Amen! :)

Why do you think God desires to use us to take care of others in this world? Why is charity important? How can we be more charitable?

329

December 22

Father God, thank You for hope. Hope is the belief that there are better times yet to come. Many times we find ourselves traveling through a tunnel, holding our breath and feeling lost, until our eye catches the light at the end of the tunnel, assuring us that this time of darkness will soon end if we would just hold on. Many times we are surrounded by chaos and destruction, tempted to believe that nothing could ever come out of the mess that we are in, but we ought to hold onto whatever we may still have, for we know that You can make beautiful things out of dust. Many times we are just tired and get tempted to give up, but forget that our breakthrough may just be an inch away, and we would reach it if we would persevere just a little bit longer. Lord, life can be a long string of unfortunate events, but may we embrace the little hope that we have that grants us the strength to keep pushing forward. In Your name we pray. Amen! :)

Why is hope important to have in this life? Do you believe that storms can and will come to an end if you would just hold on for a bit longer?

December 23

Father God, thank You for mindfulness. In a time of rush and a million things going on, it's interesting to find that some of the happiest people are the ones that live rather simple lives. Instead of falling into the lie that we need many different people, places and things in our lives, may we take the moment to stop and embrace those around us, the things we already have and the place we are already at. Instead of falling into the trap of living in either the future or the past, may we take a moment to just soak in the present time for it is not guaranteed to last and will soon be in the past. Instead of falling into the trap of taking too much on our shoulders, may we learn to say no and put our trust in You, in order to just simply be and not worry about what's not necessary. Lord, may we be more like children, content and happy no matter where they are, and mindful of the present moment. In Your name we pray. Amen! :)

Why is it important to practice mindfulness? How can you be more mindful of the present moment?

December 24

Father God, thank You for the season of Advent. Advent is the season where we get ready in anticipation of Christmas, Jesus' birth. Similar to a normal pregnancy, there are stages that must be surpassed in order to prepare for the new child to be born. Just like in Advent, receiving a baby into this world is no trivial task but requires mental and emotional preparation- therefore we must prepare our minds and hearts in order to receive Christ properly. Just like in Advent, receiving a baby requires proper planning to make room for the new bundle of joy- requiring us to declutter and clean up all the junk in our lives so that new and fresh energy can enter it. Just like in Advent, receiving a baby into this world is a joyous celebration and usually results in us sending out good cheer and excitement in all that we do- creating a new spirit about this season of receiving new life. Lord, may we embrace this new season of Advent so that we can start properly preparing our hearts, minds and homes for the birth of our Savior, Jesus. Amen! :)

How is Advent a time of preparation in your life? How can you better prepare for Advent and receiving the gift of Baby Jesus this Christmas season?

December 25

Father God, thank You for Christmas. Contrary to popular belief, Christmas is not celebrated on one day but rather every day of the year. We celebrate the birth of Your Son on the 25th but the spirit of Christmas should live within us and growing stronger with every passing day. Christmas is a reminder that the savior of the world was born and that our sins are washed away, so we should make every effort to eradicate sin in our lives. Christmas is a reminder to exercise the gifts of the Holy Spirit-gifts of peace, love, joy and hope- not only on Christmas Day but every day. Christmas is a reminder that there is meaning to all the mundane tasks we are entrusted to do while here on earth, and that we should do it unto You with all of our heart. Christmas is a reminder of all that's important in our lives, which includes our family and loved ones, and that we should tend to them for that is where our story began. Lord, help us not to lose sight of the meaning of Christmas and may we hold onto the spirit of Christmas year-round. In Your name we pray. Amen! :)

How can you celebrate Christmas every day in your life? What does that mean to you?

December 26

Father God, thank You for character. Character is the way we live, even when others are not watching. It takes years and many trials to create good character but it can be targeted and destroyed rather quickly. We should expect our character to be questioned, but we should never fret or lose our calm for we are confident that our character will speak for itself. We should expect our character to be challenged, especially during desperate times, but we should never compromise the integrity of our character but rather trust that everything will fall into place. We should expect our character to be tested, especially during times of trials and tribulations, but we should never waver our good moral standing, and trust that our character will get even stronger through the storms. Lord, may we identify the various threats on our character and stand confident in the face of attacks, challenges and tests as our character will only get stronger if we persevere. In Your name we pray. Amen! :)

Has your character ever been questioned by others? Has it ever been challenged in difficult times? How has your character spoken for itself and withstood the test of time? How can it be strengthened?

December 27

Dear God, thank You for neighbors. Neighbors are the people that we are blessed with in our lives, both near and far. It doesn't take long for us to realize that we can't do this life alone but were created for community. Neighbors can be found in our families, both immediate and extended families, and we should maintain relationship with them as much as possible to honor the blood and marriage connection that bonds each and every person. Neighbors can be found in our friends and loved ones that have made a special spot in our hearts that often times give us a reason to smile. Neighbors can be found in simply the people that live nearby, that can help us navigate through the ins and outs of the community and be there for one another in times of need. Neighbors can be found in that homeless person down the block, of whom if treated with dignity, will reciprocate the same love when given the chance or opportunity. Lord, may we recognize the neighbor in every person we meet, realizing that they are just one more link to the community that we build in our lives. In Your name we pray. Amen! :)

Who are the neighbors in your life? Do you tend to reach out to the outcasts of society? How can you love on the homeless people in town?

December 28

Father God, thank You for friendship. Friendship is that mutual relationship we share with another that satisfies an inner need in our souls. True friendship is when we are there for each other through thick and thin times, not just through fair weather when the sun is shining bright. True friendship is when we speak truth, even when it's hard to speak it, but it's something our friends need to hear. True friendship is when we accept each other for who we are without any guard or mask, with all of our flaws and scars, but are loved through it all. Lord, may we embrace the true friends that we are blessed with in our lives and may we be true friends to them as well. In Your name we pray. Amen! :)

December 29

Father God, thank you for bringing us this far in our lives. In every troubling situation, may we look back at all that we have accomplished and may it strengthen us with courage to take on the future. In Proverbs 31, a virtuous woman laughs at the future, knowing that everything will be ok. In every trial, please grant us your peace that surpasses all understanding. Allow us to meditate on your promises daily knowing that You will fulfill those promises. In this life we lead, grant us strength to persevere to the end, keeping our eyes fixated on the prize ahead of us. In Jesus' mighty name, we pray. Amen!

December 30

Father God, thank You for the "enemies" in our lives. The enemies in our lives can be anyone that we may not get along with very well or someone who has wronged us in one way or another and therefore, we harbor ill feelings toward them. It doesn't take long for us to realize that we won't get along with everyone we meet and will rub others in a wrong way, but we must still demonstrate Your love in the midst of it all. "Enemies" can be found at work in a coworker or even our boss that can make our lives more difficult, but we must find a way to show love anyways. "Enemies" can be found in people in our church and we simply don't really care for their presence but we must find a way to put our differences aside and show them love anyways. "Enemies" can be found in our families, where the people that we love the most have the capability of hurting us the most, but we must put our wounds aside and find a way to love them anyways. Lord, despite how difficult it may be, may we be strengthened to not only refuse to "hate" our enemies but rather love them and pray for them, as You would have us do. In Your name we pray. Amen! :)

Who are the "enemies" in your life? How can you love them anyways?

December 31

Father God, thank You for new beginnings. As life has its seasons, we quickly realize that we are offered many chances to start anew. These new chapters may be the end of a rough journey or a continuation of a beautiful story. These new chapters, like a book, give a whole new perspective of the story at hand, allowing us to see our lives with fresh eyes. These new chapters enable us to stop and reflect what has worked and what has not, so that we can make necessary adjustments to our future plans in order to reap the most out of life. Like a car, we see our past with a small, limited rearview mirror but look forward to the future with a large clear view through the wind shield. Lord, may we look back on the chapters that were closed as a guide that can be used for the future as we start the new unwritten chapter of our lives. In Your precious name we pray. Amen! :)

Take a moment to reflect on the past year. What was it like? What has worked and what could be better? What would you like to see changed in the new year? How will you make that happen?

Made in the USA
Columbia, SC
26 April 2019